H16n CIL

2n

TEACHING
THE MOTHER TONGUE

TEACHING THE MOTHER TONGUE

BY

PHILIP BOSWOOD BALLARD

M.A., D.Lit.

AUTHOR OF
"MENTAL TESTS," "OBLIVISCENCE AND REMINISCENCE,"
AND "HANDWORK AS AN EDUCATIONAL MEDIUM"

HODDER AND STOUGHTON
LIMITED   LONDON
1921

PREFACE

No man can in these days bring into the world a book on the teaching of English without a sense of intrusion—of invading a crowded market. So while he feels tender towards his offspring, he feels apologetic towards the world. The excuse he generally makes is either that he has new things to say, or that he puts old things in a new light. Whether I am justified in urging either of these excuses, the reader must judge for himself. One thing is certain. This book is what Edward Thring calls "a bit of life." It is beaten out of my own experience. The conclusions arrived at and the counsels offered have, in the main, been tried in the fire of experiment and confirmed by the watching of many methods applied by many minds in many schools.

No attempt is made to cover the whole field. Leaving out details of practical procedure, I content myself with enforcing basal and vital principles, with indicating what I regard as the right attitude and the right point of view, and with showing broadly the line of effort that is likely to bring in the most abundant harvest.

Roughly speaking, there are two ways of teaching English composition—the sunny way and the frosty way. This book is whole-heartedly on the side of sunshine—sunshine with a touch of frost here and there. No frost in the spring-time though! Exuberant growth should be the teacher's first concern—growth in the pupil's power to express himself freely in words; and this growth is fostered better by smiles than by frowns, better by generous praise of his successes than by cold criticism of his failures. The danger of his English growing rank and wild is less serious than is the difficulty of getting it to grow at all. Hence in this book greater stress is laid on the acquisition of positive virtues by the imitation of good models than on the acquisition of those negative virtues which consist in the mere avoidance of errors.

Another general principle that runs through the book is that of the primacy of thought. Of the two partners, thought and language, that go to produce living speech, thought is the dominant partner; and more real progress in the art of expression is gained by practice in saying vital things plainly, than by practice in saying trivial things prettily.

My attitude towards grammar needs to be more closely defined. When I speak disparagingly of grammar (as I often do), let it be understood that I always mean grammar in the narrow sense, the grammar that begins with the picking out of nouns and verbs, and ends with the parsing and analysis of a complex sentence; all the intermediate stages leading up to, and being determined by, the final flower of a perfect piece of parsing. This is what grammar meant to all teachers in the nineteenth century; this is what it means to most teachers to-day. It was the grammar that was prescribed by the Board of Education under the old system of payment by results; it was the grammar of the text-books that flourished under the shadow of that system. Finally it is the grammar whose merits and demerits I discuss in the early chapters. I there relate the story of its downfall, and try to trace the causes that led to that downfall. The tale is told in full, lest we forget; and forgetting, wish to return to those lean and lenten days when grammar took all the joy and gusto out of the English lesson, and gave no nurture in return. Few really wish to go back the whole way; but many try to go back part of the way. They call it teaching grammar incidentally.

My own solution is different. It is that in the earlier stages we should not teach grammar at all, and in the later stages teach a broader form of grammar—a form more consonant with the root meaning of the word. For grammar etymologically means the study of Letters; it means the science that lies behind the art of Literature and the practice of composition. The course of study does not lead up to parsing and analysis : it leads up to a critical examination of standard prose and standard poetry, and to the revision and correction of one's own writings. In Scotland and in America this study has never been lost. It is there called Rhetoric ; by which is meant the science of composition as distinct from the art of composition. In England the term Rhetoric has a degraded meaning. It means an art that aims at persuasion rather than proof ; and in the pursuit of that end it is suspected of using sophistry and clap-trap. That is the only reason why this book is not called The Teaching of Rhetoric.

While the early chapters deal with that narrow form of grammar which the past has discredited, the last chapter deals with that broad form of grammar which the future has yet to test. In the intermediate chapters the more practical issues are discussed.

Under a different heading, and in the guise of a series of articles, Chapters I to VIII appeared about two years ago in *The Times Educational Supplement*. To the editor of that journal my thanks are due for his kind permission to reprint the articles.

Among those with whom I have at various times discussed the topics of this book, and who have helped (not always by agreement) to mould my ideas, the following are named, no less as a tribute of friendship than as a mark of gratitude : Mr. T. Raymont, Mr. J. Nickal, Mr. G. A. Christian, Dr. A. T. de Mouilpied, Dr. J. H. Jagger, Dr. E. O. Lewis, Mr. F. P. B. Shipham, and Mr. E. J. Kenny. Most deeply am I indebted to Dr. Jagger for his thought-provoking comments, and to Mr. Kenny for his careful correction of the proofs.

I am well aware that in writing this book I am building a house of glass, and at the same time throwing a few stones—a double adventure that is not without peril. But I gladly risk the consequences, in the hope that this little book will bring to teachers in perplexity a message of help and cheer, that it will breathe more life into the dry bones of English-teaching, and that it will go some way towards making the boys and girls of England lovers of their native tongue.

P. B. BALLARD.

Chiswick,
February 1921.

CONTENTS

CONTENTS

TEACHING THE MOTHER TONGUE

CHAPTER I

THE LIMITATIONS OF GRAMMAR

(a) *Historical Background*

So prominent a place did grammar hold in the schools of the Renaissance that it gave them their distinctive title—Grammar Schools. So far has it fallen from its high estate that in many modern schools it has ceased to appear in the scheme of studies, and its very name is in danger of being forgotten. Why this loss of prestige in the subject, this change of view in the teacher —a change which, though tardy and uncertain in the secondary school, has in the primary school been both swift and sweeping?

Less than half a century ago, Matthew Arnold pressed for more and more grammar in the elementary schools; less than a quarter of a century ago children of ten were required to

B

parse every word in what was ironically called an easy sentence. The great change, like so many other great changes, began with the emancipation of 1895. Down to that date primary teachers were fettered by the syllabus laid down by the Education Department; and in that syllabus grammar bulked large, and composition occupied an inconspicuous corner. Grammar started in Standard I., and composition in Standard V. And grammar was called English—a title of honour—while composition was lumped ingloriously with handwriting and dictation. And literature was almost left out altogether. In this topsy-turvy scheme the little things were to be studied before the big things. Children had to pick out nouns before they could pick out sentences, to parse before they analyzed, to examine Shakespeare's sentences before they had read Shakespeare's plays.

Looking back upon the practice of those days, we see nothing that compels us to believe that grammar as a branch of study is unsuited for the young; but we find abundant evidence that it can be wrongly conceived and badly taught. Indeed, the first reform that followed the emancipation of the teacher was a reform in the method of teaching the subject. The sentence, rather than the word, now became the starting-point. Analysis took precedence over parsing, both in order of sequence and in order of importance. Grammatical terminology was simplified, and a better understanding of the functions of words was aimed at. It was more and more clearly realized that language comes first and grammar second; and that the rules of grammar, far from being consciously formulated laws that regulate the growth and use of language, either in the race or in the child, are simply uniformities that are discovered in the language after it has already grown. A certain orderliness is manifest in the usages of speech, and grammar is a study of that orderliness. It was remembered that Plato never saw a Greek grammar, and Shakespeare never an English one. The prevalence of this view led to a reversing of the rôles of grammar and composition. Instead of beginning grammar at seven and composition at eleven, pupils now began composition at seven and grammar at eleven. And literature began to come into its own. English no longer meant grammar; it meant mainly, and it meant primarily, literature and composition. And with the extended cultivation of the mother tongue in book, speech and script, there grew in the teacher's mind a steady conviction that grammar, whether well taught or ill taught, was, in respect of intelligibility and force of appeal, far inferior to the study of the living language as a vehicle of song or story. And far less useful. Indeed, its suitability in any guise for children in elementary schools began to be a matter of doubt; and the question whether grammar should be taught at all became, for the first time in the history of pedagogy, an intelligible and pertinent question.

Then came, in 1905, the *Suggestions to Teachers*, with its refreshing chapter on the Teaching of English, probably the most revolutionary chapter in a revolutionary book. And it preached the new view. "Until a child," it asserts, "has learnt to think consecutively and to express his thoughts clearly, he has no basis for that formal study of language which is called grammar." "With the younger scholars it should be discontinued altogether." The gist of the new doctrine was incorporated in subsequent issues of the Code. This is the passage: "Instruction in grammar should be confined to the higher classes. If given, it should be directed to enabling the scholars to understand the structure of the sentences which they speak, read, or write, and the functions of the several words in those sentences, and should be as free as possible from technicalities." The phrase "if given" strongly suggested that it need not be given at all; and by a large number of teachers it was so interpreted. The result was that the subject began to disappear from the school curriculum.

In London the next stage was marked by the publication, in 1909, of the L.C.C. Report of the Conference on the Teaching of English in London Elementary Schools. Here a strong attempt was made to stem the tide of professional opinion, and to restore to grammar some of its lost prestige. "Our opinion is unanimous," says the Report, "that some amount of definite grammatical instruction, varying with circumstances and aptitudes, must be given to our scholars." It recommended that the systematic study of the subject should begin as early as nine years of age; and in spite of its rejection of the old machinery of parsing and analysis, compared with the "Suggestions" the document was distinctly pro-grammar. Its avowed aim was to find a *via media* between the old order and the new. As a step it was a step back towards the starting-point.

So, in fact, was the issue in 1915 of a revised edition of the "Suggestions," although in this case the step was a very small one. The rigour of the earlier scepticism was abated, and it was conceded that the formal teaching of grammar could not wholly be abandoned. Without committing itself to a commencing age, it broadly indicated the minimum of grammar that a child should know before leaving the elementary school. As a whole, however, the tenour of its teaching was unchanged. Grammar was given a much less important place in the school economy than was contemplated in the L.C.C. Report.

In the schools, meanwhile, practice varied and opinion vacillated. The only point of unanimity was the abandonment of the old programme. Nobody taught the subject in the old order; nobody taught it with the old thoroughness. It was either not taught at all, or taught with the avowed object of helping the composition. By the rejection of all that the pupil could not directly apply to his own speech or script, an attempt was made to reduce the scheme of grammatical study to a minimum. But on the nature and amount of that minimum there was the widest difference of opinion.

So far the ordinary elementary schools. In schools for higher education the problems became more numerous, more complex, and more thorny. Where the pupil speaks no language but his own, it is perhaps possible to dispense with the study of grammar, but where he has to learn another language, the grammar problem acquires a new significance and a new import. For it is not a simple question of grammar or no grammar, since in these schools the necessity for grammar has never been challenged, but rather a question of priority, of amount, and of co-ordination. Is the study of the fundamental grammatical relationships best approached, as our forefathers thought, through a highly inflected language like Latin, where those relationships stand out clearly and arrestingly, or through the mother tongue, where inflexions are few but usage is familiar ? As for modern languages, even the most ardent advocates of the direct method of teaching disagree respecting the stage at which grammar should be introduced and the amount that it is expedient to teach. The different grammatical terminology, too, used in different languages proved a fruitful source of confusion. On this point reform was unanimously demanded. It was clear that consistency and economy of thought called for consistency and economy of nomenclature. To meet this demand a Joint Committee on Grammatical Terminology was appointed in 1909. The next year they published their report, which indeed helped to remove one of the anomalies of instruction in grammar, but left the most vital problems untouched.

And this was the situation when the Great War came upon us. In the secondary school the teaching of grammar was struggling towards stability ; in the elementary school it was fighting for its very existence.

CHAPTER II

(b) *The Utilitarian Plea*

LEAVING the manifold problems of secondary education, let us address ourselves to the simpler task of considering why English grammar is taught at all in the elementary schools.

The reason generally given by its modern apologists is a utilitarian reason : it is claimed to be useful in teaching composition. Do not our old grammarians define grammar as the art of speaking and writing with propriety ? Is it not the common, if not the universal, belief that bad English is due to ignorance of grammar ? If so, the first question we have to answer is, To what extent does instruction in grammar help children in the elementary schools to express themselves clearly and accurately ? This is not a matter on which we need appeal to authority, unless indeed it be to the inexorable authority of facts. We have only to compare the composition in a grammar-ridden school with a composition in a grammarless school. At the beginning of the century, examples of these two types of school were frequently found in the same neighbourhood, attended by the same class of children, taught by the same kind of teacher—similar, in fact, in all respects save that literature in the one took the place of grammar in the other. And it is the emphatic verdict of all who had an opportunity of examining and comparing the work of these schools that the composition was incontestably better in the grammarless schools. But one need not compare different schools : one can compare results of the two systems in one and the same school. Many a head teacher of to-day has conducted his school definitely from one stage to the other—from the grammar stage to the grammarless. And his opinion neither hesitates nor varies : as the grammar got less, the composition got better. And although it may be urged that this improvement is due not so much to the incident that grammar was dropped, as to the accession of certain positive elements, still the fact remains that the dropping of grammar has at least not prevented the improvement. What in the old days the teacher failed to achieve with grammar is now achieved without it.

It may, however, be contended, and justly contended, that the evidence we have so far adduced falls far short of proving that grammar is useless ; at the most it only proves that it is less useful than literature. And if we had no other kind of evidence, the case against the usefulness of grammar would be presumptive merely. But we have another kind of evidence. It is afforded by the researches of Mr. F. S. Hoyt,[1] an American, who argues that if the study of formal grammar helps children to use good English, then those who excel in grammar will, as a general rule, excel in composition, and those who are weak in the one will be weak in the other. As the reader is doubtless aware, there is a mathematical device, known as the method of correlation, which enables us to determine the exact relationship between two kinds of ability. Mr. Hoyt employed this device to compare the attainments in grammar on the one hand, and composition on the other, of 200 Indianapolis high-school pupils who had just completed a common course of study at the elementary schools. Each paper was marked independently by two examiners. One examiner found a correlation of ·12 and the other a correlation of ·23. These tests were repeated in the schools of Minneapolis by Mr. R. W. Rapeer, who also found a correlation of ·23. We may safely assume, therefore, that the true correlation is not higher than ·3. What does this mean ? It means that there is less connexion

[1] See the *Journal of Educational Psychology*, iv. 3, pp. 125–137.

between grammar and composition than Dr. Bradford and Dr. Carey have found to exist between handwriting and science, between needlework and geography, and between arithmetic and spelling.[1] It means that the chances of anybody who is good at grammar being also good at composition are only about 6 in 10. But this degree of probability may reasonably be expected of any two kinds of ability taken at random: it is no more than can be accounted for by assuming in each pupil a central fund of general intelligence. If there were a causal nexus between the two specific factors, the correlation would be much higher. In other words, if the doctrine of correlation is sound, it is just as reasonable for children of thirteen to practise needlework in order to improve their geography as to study grammar in order to improve their composition.

A suspicion will here cross the reader's mind that we are confusing two distinct things—good English and correct English; that we are expecting the study of grammar to do more than it claims to do. Nobody maintains that grammar will give the child ideas, or that it will give him words in which to express his ideas; few will maintain that it will enable him to arrange his ideas clearly and logically. What is claimed

[1] See *The Distribution and Relation of Educational Abilities*, by Cyril Burt, p. 61.

is that grammar will enable him to express his ideas correctly—to express them in accordance with established custom. Its function is, in fact, neither to vivify nor to fructify, but to regulate. It gives nothing; it merely moulds and modifies. And if we have been judging the merit of composition by its substance rather than by its grammatical form, by the ideas and the fitness of the phraseology rather than by the correctness of accidence and syntax, then the argument would seem to fail of its purpose. It would still remain to be proved that the study of grammar does not help the young pupil to speak grammatically. In point of fact, however, it does not matter what aspect of composition is tested; in no case has it been found to be benefited by the study of formal grammar.

The actual effect of grammar upon speech may readily be ascertained by the reader if he be a teacher or have access to an elementary school where grammar is being taught. Let him seek, as I have often sought, clear, indisputable instances where pupils have rectified solecisms by their knowledge of grammar, instances where they have consciously applied this knowledge to the checking of a bad linguistic habit or to the resolution of cases of doubt. If he finds one incontestable instance he will have succeeded where most inquirers have failed. Let him probe the minds of a number of children—children who can parse and analyze with facility—to discover what they really think of such a sentence as " Come for a walk with John and me." He will find that they can neither justify it nor discuss it. They invariably say that it is wrong, and vote for " John and I." But, whether they say it is right or wrong, they can never give reasons for their opinion that are in any sense grammatical. Even in the simplified form " Come for a walk with me " they fail to justify the use of " me " rather than " I." When driven to a corner they reveal the real ground of their opinion—the phrase sounds right, or it sounds wrong. If, therefore, when challenged and pressed to apply their knowledge of grammar to a simple case, they so signally fail, what reason have we to hope that they will spontaneously apply it in the common intercourse of life ?

There are other forms of the utilitarian argument. It is asserted, for instance, that the teacher finds it difficult, if not impossible, to correct his pupils' errors in speaking and writing unless he can refer to these errors in technical terms. We are asked to believe that when a lad is told that he has been guilty of false concord, he will understand his error better than when told that he has used words which do not agree—which do not go well together ; and that we help him more by informing him that he has used a past participle as a finite verb than by simply saying that he has used the wrong word. The grammatical labels are supposed to economize time and effort. But the value of these labels depends on their intelligibility. When they are unintelligible, or even dimly understood, they are worse than useless; worse because they bar the way to an intelligible explanation. And grammatical terminology is never so clearly apprehended by pre-adolescents that its relevancy to a case in point jumps to the mind. To them it is an explanation that does not explain. It is, in fact, an attempt to get them over a difficulty by obtruding on their notice a still greater difficulty.

The utilitarian defence takes yet another form —that of asserting that grammar helps the pupil to understand the writings of others, that it has an interpretative value. This plea is based on pure conjecture. When put to the test it breaks down. Hoyt and Rapeer, in the research referred to above, included a test in interpretation; and they found the correlation between grammar and interpretation to be just as low as that between grammar and composition.

It is seen, therefore, that the belief in the usefulness of grammar to elementary school children has not much support in fact. I have given reasons for thinking that correct English is not acquired by the young through the study of grammatical rules. But this is only half the argument. The other half consists in showing how, in point of fact, correct English is acquired. This task I will attempt in a later chapter.

CHAPTER III

THE LIMITATIONS OF GRAMMAR (*continued*)

(c) *Disciplinary Pleas*

MOST teachers of experience have realized that the practical effect of instruction in grammar on the speech of the young is so small as to be negligible. They find it necessary, therefore, to put forward some other plea for the inclusion of the subject in the programme of studies. And the plea they generally urge is the cultural plea: grammar is claimed to be a valuable means of mental discipline. Miss Brackenbury, in her admirable little book on the teaching of grammar, says: " Grammar is an instrument of special value to the teacher, as it affords him unique opportunities of getting his pupils to think." And again: " The teaching of grammar cannot, therefore, be justified on the ground that the facts acquired are of direct practical value; it is justified on the ground that the subject-matter affords us a unique means of getting the child to see fine distinctions." The very justification which is rejected in *Suggestions to Teachers*, and

which is given a subordinate place in the L.C.C
Report, is in Miss Brackenbury's book held to be
not merely the strongest justification, but the
only justification. Moreover, a certain unique-
ness is claimed for it.

Before we can discuss this point we must ourselves make a distinction between the ground for
selecting a branch of school study and the aim
the teacher has in view while teaching it. It is
a matter of historical fact that no school subject
has ever been selected for its disciplinary value,
and it is a matter of demonstrable theory that no
school subject ever should be selected on that
ground. Subjects have got into the school
because they have met some social demand; the
disciplinary plea has always been an after-thought
—a last line of defence fallen back upon when
every other line has broken down. The truth
is that mental discipline does not depend upon
subject-matter, but upon the way in which that
subject-matter is mastered. It is sometimes a
question of good teaching; always a question of
right learning. Thring defends the classics as
the best means of making pupils think. Dewey
defends handwork on precisely the same plea.
Mathematics, science, composition, geography—
indeed, every subject that has found a footing in
the school—has been claimed by some one or
other as a unique means of making the pupils

c

think. Professor Adams, in ironic mood, has suggested burglary and petty larceny as affording excellent opportunities for mind-training. But although we cannot accept the alleged thought-compelling power of a subject as giving it right of entry into the curriculum, the true teacher feels in every fibre that the success of his teaching depends upon the extent to which he has utilized that thought-compelling power. Hard thinking (by the pupil, not the teacher) is the touchstone of a good lesson. And to this extent Miss Brackenbury is right : that if grammar be taught at all, it should be taught with the constant purpose of encouraging thought. But then she would not teach it at all to young children. " It is studied," she says, " with most advantage between the ages of fourteen and sixteen." She would therefore agree that, on whatever grounds grammar is taught, if taught before the pupil has reached adolescence it is taught prematurely.

Lurking in the disciplinary defence lie two inveterate fallacies. One is that the harder a subject is, the better it is as a means of mental training, and the other is that thinking in one sphere of thought is precisely the same thing as thinking in any other sphere of thought. That a certain degree of difficulty is necessary to evoke a desirable effort, will readily be conceded ; but the effort must be within the capacity of the pupil, and the conquest of the difficulty must appear to him to be worth while. Achievement must appeal to him as being both expedient and possible. If the friction be too great, it will stop the machine. The suitability of a subject as a provoker of thought evidently depends on the preparedness of the pupil. If he is not interested in the subject, and cannot by reasonably good teaching be made interested in it, it clearly indicates that he is not yet ready for it. For if he is not interested in it he has no appetite for it, and if he has no appetite for it he will not digest it, and if he will not digest it it will do him more harm than good. That elementary school children are not interested in grammar is a demonstrable fact. Of all the subjects in the curriculum it is the most unpopular. If we find the popularity of a subject varying from school to school and from class to class, we may suspect differences of skill on the part of the teachers to be the cause of the variation, and no inference can be drawn respecting the intrinsic attractiveness of the subject ; but when we find the subject greatly disliked in every school, in every class, and by each sex, we have just grounds for believing the subject itself to be incompatible with childish interests. And this is precisely what is true of grammar. In 1913 Dr. E. O. Lewis conducted an inquiry into the popularity of school subjects, and found that grammar was universally disliked. It always came at the bottom of the list.

The L.C.C. Report asserts that in the days of rigid departmental examinations grammar was probably the most unpopular subject in the curriculum, and ascribes its unpopularity to the fact that it was taught for its own sake and was thereby divorced from the pleasanter and more humanizing phases of English study. Nay, it was not *probably* the most unpopular subject, it was *certainly* so. And it is not merely of the past that it is true; it is true to-day, with its more enlightened teaching and its strenuous efforts to connect grammar with speaking, reading and writing. Dr. Lewis's research was carried out in 1913, when the old-fashioned methods had long been discarded. As late as April 1918, I visited a higher grade boys' school where the Head Master believed that boys liked grammar, and we put the matter to the test in the way suggested by Dr. Lewis. We selected the highest class but one, and got each boy to arrange in order of preference the sixteen subjects upon which separate lessons were given. The ordinal number of the subject was regarded as so many votes, the total number of the votes for each subject thus affording an inverse measure of its popularity. History came first with 169 votes, and grammar last with 512. If handicraft had been taken (war conditions had temporarily excluded it) it would probably have competed with history for the first place. No other subject came within fifty votes of grammar in point of unpopularity. Here we have a class of intellectuals—the best brains from the surrounding elementary schools—children who take French, and place it fifth in order of preference, who take science, and place it second ; and if they can take no interest in grammar, can we reasonably expect it of the children in the ordinary elementary school ? The boys were asked to give reasons. This is one : " I do not like grammar because it is absolutely dry." The word " dry " was underlined thrice. More illuminating still is the reason given by one of Dr. Lewis's boys : " I don't like grammar because I am not good at guessing." I have repeated this experiment in many other schools, and always with the same result. Grammar always came last.

As for the second implication (that of thinking that one's wits sharpened on one kind of material are thereby rendered keen for acting on every other kind of material), that is the old doctrine of formal training, which nobody can now accept without being blind to a large mass of adverse evidence which has been accumulating for the last twenty years.

It is worthy of note that if we leave out of

consideration the fitness of the subject for the
pupil's stage of mental development—which is
really the crux of the question—every argument
that has been used to justify the teaching of
grammar in elementary schools may be applied
with still greater cogency to the teaching of logic.
If it is desirable that a child should speak correctly, it is much more desirable that he should
think correctly. Right thinking is prior to right
speaking, and more fundamental. And the laws
that regulate the processes of thought have a
stronger claim on the teacher than the laws that
regulate the use of language. And how can a
teacher rectify the faulty reasoning of a child
unless he can refer each blunder to its proper
group—can call one a case of undistributed
middle, another a case of *ignoratio elenchi*, and
another a case of *petitio principii?* About the
practical value of instruction in logic there can
therefore, be no doubt. And as for its disciplinary
value, what subject is better fitted to bring into
play the higher processes of thought than that
concerned with the very validity of thought
itself ?

An equally strong claim may be made out for
the study of ethics in the elementary school.
Does not every book on education, including
the Government Code, lay it down as an irrefut-
able principle that the primary aim of education

is the moral aim ? And should our children study so subsidiary a thing as language and neglect so important a thing as conduct ? And how can we call attention to moral lapses without referring to the categorical imperative, or pointing out the inadequacy of utilitarian motives, or telling the delinquent that he has failed to realize his rational self ? And as for the mental discipline that consists in discerning fine distinctions, what field affords so large an opportunity ? Yet nobody has ever suggested that we should introduce the formal study of logic or of ethics into the elementary school. We are not ashamed to let the children go out into the world ignorant of the fact that such subjects exist.

We may admit, therefore, the fundamental importance of grammar, we may admit its practical value, we may admit its value as a means of mental discipline ; but unless we can show that it is suited to the understanding of children under fourteen years of age, we have failed to make good its claim to a place in the curriculum of the elementary school.

CHAPTER IV

THE LIMITATIONS OF GRAMMAR (*continued*)

(d) *How a Child Learns to Speak*

WHEN we consider the large number of subtle relationships of thought that find expression in changes in the form and sequence of words; how low a ratio the number of wrong uses bears to the number of right uses, even in the speech of the most uncultured; especially when we consider that a child of five, within the limits of his knowledge, speaks his own tongue with greater fluency and correctness than an educated foreigner who has spent many hours of toil over an English grammar—when we remember all this, we cannot but marvel at the potency of natural forces in moulding the usages of speech. How does a child learn to speak correctly? In precisely the same way that he learns to speak at all—by imitation of his elders. If he listens to good models he will speak well, if to bad models he will speak badly.

But imitation is not the only process at work. The human mind, however immature or primitive it may be, is never merely reproductive : it is constructive as well. There is much parrot-work in learning to speak; but it is not all parrot-work. A child of tender years will some-times use words that he has never heard, will often frame sentences which are entirely his own. A peculiar subconscious process has been at work. The young mind tends to press new words into old forms that have become habitual, without in any way being able to disentangle the form from the filling. " I finked it in my head," was the remark of a boy of four. Is it to be believed that he generalized from past tenses of weak verbs, and consciously applied the old rule to the new instance ? To give other samples of infantile speech : " You'd rather me come to meet you, daddy, rathern't you ? " " You'll be able to come, be-able-n't you ? " It is impossible to believe that these curious words are due to imitation, for adults never use them. It is equally impossible to believe that the children who used them consciously reasoned by analogy from such words as couldn't, wouldn't, and shouldn't. We are forced to assume some general-izing mechanism at work below the surface. It enables the growing child to absorb new words into his vocabulary and to use them rightly : to give the noun its right number, the verb its right tense, the words their right order, and the sentence its right structure. Just as a very young child can recognize his father without being able to name a single mark of recognition, just as he can walk without knowing anything about the system of levers which moves his limbs, so can he feel that a certain grammatical form is right, and that another form is wrong, without being able to give any sort of explanation. If pressed for a reason he can never get beyond saying that the words sound right or that they sound wrong.

It is neither more nor less wonderful than the way in which a child learns the meanings of words. An intelligent lad, long before he reaches puberty, although he may never have asked the meaning of a single word, never have consulted a dictionary, never have tried of set purpose to learn the correct use and purport of either word or phrase, will yet have good command of a vocabulary which is the very pith and marrow of his mother tongue. The sounds of the words he can learn by imitation; but their meaning can only be mastered by much sifting and comparing and inferring—not with deliberate effort, but by a process as easy and natural as breathing. Just as the meanings of words are learnt without a dictionary—and learnt better without a dictionary—so is grammatical usage learnt without a grammar—and learnt better without a grammar. The precise nature of this subconscious process has never been fully discovered; largely for the reason that it *is* subconscious. Stout, in his *Analytic Psychology*, describes analogous processes under the term " relative suggestion." The phrase " subconscious inference " has been used by some and objected to by others ; not that these others deny the fact, but that they deny the appropriateness of calling any process inference which does not take place in the full light of thought.

To avoid this war of words let us label the unconscious method of learning the natural method, and the deliberate and systematic search for principles the pedagogic method. And let us note the points of difference between the two. For they are many. One is easy, the other difficult ; one is employed at every stage of mental development, the other either not at all or at the later stages only ; one is applied rapidly and easily, the other slowly and hesitatingly ; one gives rise to language that is largely automatic, the other promotes self-consciousness and a halting habit of speech ; one sets the mind free to fix upon the meaning, the other diverts the mind from the meaning and pins it to the expression. Whatever formal means be adopted by an adult to acquire a new language, however much he rely on the pedagogic method of dictionary and grammar, if he is to speak and write the language with any measure of facility he must apply his rules unwittingly; he must, that is, reach by a circuitous route the very goal to which the natural method leads direct. The only grammar we can use in discursive speech is either the grammar we have never learnt, or the grammar we have learnt and forgotten—forgotten, at least, at the moment of its use. For to speak any language, whether native or foreign, entirely by rule, is quite impossible. The rule distracts attention from the sense, and takes too long a time to apply. By the time the speaker has remembered the rule he has forgotten what he had to say. In fluent speech the words take their proper forms and fall into their proper places in accordance with a slowly acquired habit. And they do so with that precision, automatism, and economy of effort which habit always ensures. It is clear, then, why the attempt to rectify grammatical errors by rule is so signally ineffective. It is pitting the pedagogic method against the natural method, opposing a weak artificial force to a strong natural force, trying with a bucket to turn aside a stream. I refer, of course, to the young. As the pupil gets older the pedagogic method gains potency and can be made a valuable helper and corrector of the natural method. But with quite young children the pedagogic method has no potency at all. For part of its force depends upon its being understood, and the rest upon the capacity of the pupil to apply it ; and young children fail, as a rule, to understand it, and when, as an exception, they seem to understand it, they fail to apply it.

But if children learn to speak correctly by imitation, how do they learn to speak incorrectly ? By imitation too. As a general rule, the correct form to the child is the form he most frequently hears. It is beaten into his mind by constant reiteration. If a child always hears " done " and " seen " used as past tenses, he accepts them on trust, as he accepts all other vocables. He has no more ground for suspecting the correctness of " I done it " than he has for suspecting the correctness of " I won it." It is only when he hears conflicting usages that suspicion can possibly arise. What happens then depends largely on the degree of fixity of the prior habit. With quite young children the habits of speech are very unstable. And fortunately so. Their first attempts to imitate the words and phrases used by others are tentative and temporary. " No," for instance, may become the universal negative. " Me no like brush hair " is found by many a child to express with sufficient clearness his protest against one of his mother's ministrations. But if he hears adults express this differently, he does not continue to say it for long. He is constantly readjusting his language to bring it nearer the standard presented to him day after day. When they correspond exactly he adjusts no longer, and begins to indurate. His linguistic habits, for good or ill, begin to set and harden. And the longer and more frequently they are practised, the more difficult are they to eradicate. The teacher in the slum school knows only too well how unequal is the match between him and the pupils' home environment. He tries by dint of constant correction and a little grammar to improve their speech ; and when he succeeds he ascribes it to the grammar. "Incantation and arsenic," says Voltaire, " will kill a flock of sheep." The pedagogic mind is apt to put its trust in the abracadabra of grammar, while the arsenic of habit does the work.

Can anybody really believe that a child of ten who uses " done " instead of " did " (to return to the most inveterate solecism to which London children are addicted) can be made to use the right word by having it driven into him that " done " is a past participle and " did " the past indefinite tense of the finite verb ? As the mistake was never reasoned into him, so will it never be reasoned out of him. The phrase " I done it " has already become part and parcel of the mind's deepest structure, and the teacher's hardest task is not to make the child realize its wrongness (that is by no means difficult : the child will readily accept the fact on the mere *ipse dixit* of the teacher), but to make that knowledge organic—to get the wrong phrase out of the under-mind and to get the right phrase in. It is not a matter of surface consciousness, but of subconsciousness ; not a matter of intelligence, but of habit. The two factors may indeed conflict, as is illustrated by the case of the schoolboy who said, " Please, teacher, Tom has put ' putten ' where he should have putten ' put.' "

In his contest with the influence of street and home the teacher has one strong point in his favour—the weight of his scholastic authority. What has been said above about the frequency with which the learner hears grammatical forms, needs some qualification. The instances have to be weighed as well as counted. The more respect the child has for his linguistic model, the deeper will be the impression he receives. The right form uttered once by his teacher may outweigh the wrong form uttered a dozen times by his playmate.

CHAPTER V

(e) *The Difficulty of Grammar*

THE difficulty of grammar is the difficulty that lies at the root of all philosophical studies—that of regarding familiar things from an unfamiliar point of view. It is like looking at one's glasses instead of looking through them. The subject-matter of grammar is language, and to a young child language is a tool to be used rather than an object to be examined. But although the essential subject-matter of grammar is language, it is not language pure and simple ; it is language in relation to two other orders of existence—to thoughts on the one hand, and things on the other. It expresses thoughts ; it refers to things. Thus there has to be kept before the mind of the pupil a threefold series, with the word-series forming the base at which his attention is predominantly fixed and to which it must constantly return. An adjective, for instance, is a word, and yet it describes a thing. Mood is a form of a word, and yet it indicates a relationship between a thought and an action. This shifting of attention from one category to another, preserving at the same time its centre of gravity within the category of words, is a balancing feat to which the immature mind is quite unaccustomed. A child's natural proclivity of mind is towards things. He finds it hard to think about words, harder still to think about thoughts, hardest of all to think about relationships between thoughts, words and things. He is mainly concerned with, and interested in, the world as objective, as external; and language is to him a medium by which his thoughts about it may be organized. And a transparent medium. Scarcely aware of the medium itself, he gazes through it at the meaning behind. It is in this meaning, especially as it bears on the ever-changing panorama of life, that his interest lies; it is here alone that his attention finds a reasonable measure of stability. When words themselves become part of the panorama, when they are stripped bare of their ordinary relations of meaning and function, when they become mere curiosities of sound without sense, when, in fine, words become things, he can then be made to take considerable interest in them. A young lad loves to ask: How much wood would a woodchuck chuck if a woodchuck could chuck wood? without in the least knowing or even caring what a woodchuck is. Nor is he in quest of statistical

D

information, for he supplies the solution himself. As much wood as a woodchuck would chuck if a woodchuck could chuck wood. It is when we invite him to attend to the function of words—to the relationships between them and their meanings—it is then that his attention flags and fails.

Even the very distinction between words and things he finds by no means easy to grasp; to maintain the distinction for any length of time he finds impossible. His mind ever tends to slip back to its customary pose—to the familiar outward-looking attitude. Questioning a class of boys, an inspector asked: "If you were to say to me, 'You was here yesterday,' would that be right?" "No, Sir!" was the reply. "And why not?" "Please, Sir, because you wasn't." It was the fact that seemed important to these boys, not the form in which the fact was expressed. They generally fail to distinguish a solecism from a lie, a vulgarism from a fallacy, an error of form from an error of meaning.

That children find a difficulty in discriminating between words and things, is not to be wondered at, for adults find the same difficulty. Grammarians themselves, at the very point where it is most important to preserve the distinction (that is, in the definitions), are frequently found tripping. The definition of "case" is a great stumbling-block; so is that of "a preposition."

Both are often said to indicate relationships between words, whereas, of course, they really indicate relationships between things. Dr. Morris and Mr. Nesfield, to take, almost at random, two modern authorities of recognized standing, not infrequently confuse the categories. Thus Morris defines case as " that form of the noun (or pronoun) which shows its relation to some other word in the sentence "; and Nesfield says, " The relation in which a noun stands to some other word, or the change of form (if any) by which this relation is indicated, is called its case." Even at the outset, the two grammarians differ; for Morris defines a sentence as a complete thought put into words, while Nesfield defines it as a combination of words that makes a complete sense. Is a sentence essentially a thought, or is it a string of words? The truth is that it is a compound of the two, and it depends on our point of view which we regard as the essential element. Morris takes the standpoint of the logician, Nesfield that of the grammarian.

In addition to the difficulty of deflecting attention to unaccustomed angles, of dragging into the full light of consciousness what usually lies in shadow, and of making distinctions which, as they serve no practical purpose, seem to the young to be idle and gratuitous, there is yet another difficulty inherent in the subject-matter itself; and that is its arbitrariness, its refusal to fall under universal rules. About the laws of Nature there is a certain inevitableness. They are both uniform and universal. The seeming exception is not a real exception. A closer scrutiny shows that instead of violating the law—if it be a true law—it serves to verify and confirm it ; which, indeed, is the only real sense in which the exception proves the rule. And even in grammar, or rather in what has been called general or universal grammar, there are similar uniformities. For as there are certain laws of thought which are common to all mankind, independent of race or education, so are there certain laws of verbal expression which are common to all languages, native or foreign, living or dead. But in the grammar peculiar to each language, in the inflexions of words and their order of sequence, there is a certain freakishness which disconcerts the learner and sometimes sets him wondering whether rules are of any use at all. Why, for instance, should " mouse " form its plural in one way and " house " in another ? Why should not " freeze " and " sneeze " form their past tenses alike ? Yet what uniformity there is, is better than none ; unless, indeed, it be that mentioned by Heine when he said that irregular verbs are distinguished from the regular verbs by the fact that in learning them one gets more whippings.

So intractable is the material that definition,

which in the exact sciences is so important, is
here almost impossible. Some grammarians give
up the task as hopeless and make no attempt
at strictly defining their terms. When they
do attempt it they frequently fail. What, for
instance, is a personal pronoun? And what a
relative? I have never seen a definition of
either which is not open to some objection. I
cannot better illustrate this point than by quot-
ing from the Report of the Joint Committee
on Grammatical Terminology one of the few
attempts at definition that appear therein. It
is this: "The traditional term 'relative' is, of
course, inadequate; words like 'who,' 'which,'
differ from other pronouns by marking the clause
or sentence which they introduce as forming part
of a larger group." What meaning can we
attach to this extraordinary dictum? What is
the larger group of which the clause or sentence
forms part? Logically, it can only mean a
larger group of clauses or sentences. But every
subordinate clause, whatever the introductory
word, forms part of a larger group of clauses
which together make up the complex sentence.
And every sentence in continuous prose forms
part of a larger group of sentences which constitute a paragraph. This is, therefore, a definition
which does not define, and a proposal to replace
an inadequacy by an absurdity.

As the surface meaning is inadmissible, we must

seek for another. It seems probable that the Committee intended merely to say that a relative pronoun limits—that the group denoted by the antecedent is larger than, and includes, the group denoted by the relative. But this is only sometimes true, not always. To take two lines from Tennyson's *Ulysses*, it is true of one ("I am a part of all that I have met"), and false of the other ("And see the great Achilles, whom we knew"). In the latter instance, indeed, there is neither group nor limitation. It follows that, on the most generous interpretation, the proposal is to substitute for one inadequacy another which is still greater. If, therefore, a body of eminent scholars, meeting together to consider the question of grammatical terminology, can bungle so over a common part of speech, are we not justified in suspecting the suitability of the subject for children of tender years? [1]

[1] This criticism led to a correspondence between Professor E. A. Sonnenschein and myself in *The Times Educational Supplement*, beginning with the issue of February 20, 1919. Professor Sonnenschein pointed out that the words quoted by me were taken from the provisional, and not from the final Report (a fact of which I was not at the time aware); that they were not intended as a definition; and that they merely meant "that the pronouns and adjectives called relative are connective." I give the defence without comment, beyond remarking that the correspondence that ensued was itself evidence in support of my view that the study of grammar is unsuited for young minds.

CHAPTER VI

THE LIMITATIONS OF GRAMMAR (*continued*)

(f) *The Informal Study of Language*

LET us bear clearly in mind the real points at issue. They are two only. The first is, When should grammar be taught? and the second, How should it be approached? Of the educational value of grammar itself there can be no doubt. It is not against the teaching of grammar that objections have been raised, but against the premature teaching of grammar and the bad teaching of grammar.

When, then, is it premature? Careful observation and experiment point to the beginning of adolescence, that is, about the age of twelve, as the stage previous to which grammar makes no appeal whatever. The young pupil takes no interest in it : he fails to understand it. The only excuse for forcing it upon him at all is its supposed influence upon the language he uses. But the supposition has been shown to be groundless. There is no more reason for thinking that the ability to identify parts of speech affects a child's English, than there is for thinking that the ability to identify molars affects the mastication of his food. Before the age of twelve the study of grammar is demonstrably premature. Between the ages of twelve and fourteen the study of the subject is possible, but scantily productive. Sparse indeed is the crop, even when the ground is well tilled and the seed well sown. But despite the meagre outcome, there was under the old régime much to be said for the teaching of grammar to all children before they reached the age of fourteen—before they went forth into the world and abandoned, as most of them did, the paths of study for ever. That no child should leave school ignorant of the existence of a subject called grammar, nor of the grammatical terms in common use, is what most schoolmasters have felt : and few have dared, even in the poorest of schools, to rid the curriculum entirely of grammar. But the new Education Act has changed the perspective. Fourteen is no longer a terminus ; it is merely a junction. And the now-or-never argument no longer holds good. In fact there are good grounds for holding the view that in future formal grammar is a subject to be taught, not in the elementary school, but in the continuation school.

The plan now prevailing in many elementary schools is to use a series of class text-books, called by some such title as Lessons in English or

Language Lessons. But these text-books, promising as they may seem at first glance, prove to be just as unfruitful as the old-fashioned parsing and analysis. And no wonder : for they are, in fact, grammar-books in disguise. Their aim is to identify and label the various parts of a sentence and to explain grammatical relationships. It is true that their method is good. The rules are arrived at inductively through an abundance of examples, and frequent opportunities are given for applying the rules to new instances. And if grammar is to be taught at all, there is no better way of teaching it. Yet it must be admitted that this text-book system has signally failed. In no school are the books studied from cover to cover. A selection is always made, generally scanty, frequently haphazard, always defeating the aim and purport of the series.

If, then, the best modern substitute for the ancient gerund-grinding has broken down, how are we to deal with the pre-grammar period ? Are we to make no attempt in the elementary school to rescue the children from the dialect of the streets ? Nay, but we must cease to use ineffectual means, and learn to use those that palpably succeed. We must rely upon imitation as our main standby, with an appeal, when possible, to common sense. In discussing with the pupils the rightness or wrongness of an expression, the best criteria to apply are those which they naturally possess. Of these the commonest is congruity with what has been heard in the past : does the phrase sound right or does it sound wrong? And indeed this is the criterion by which adults judge in nine cases out of ten. If we are in doubt whether the past tense of " spring " is " sprang " or " sprung," we try it in a sentence. We compare " he sprang into the air " with " he sprung into the air," and we trust our ear. Few if any of us have learnt by rote the principal parts of English verbs in the form of " spring, sprang, sprung," as a foreigner learns them. Yet we can use them with much greater facility and certainty than the foreigner by simply adopting the form that sounds right. The principle will not carry us all the way, even with adults ; still less with young barbarians who, having had their ears attuned to ungrammatical expressions, judge by a vitiated standard. But although not all the way, it will carry us a long way. For an analysis of grammatical errors will reveal the fact that the bulk of them are due to the disturbing influence of contiguous words. None but the most illiterate will use a plural verb with a singular subject unless some disturbing phrase intervenes between the subject and its predicate. To bring the disagreement to the clear apprehension of the pupil, all one has to do is to remove temporarily the misguiding words. The following sentences, for example, are such as are frequently found in children's writings. Remove the words in italics and the blunder stands revealed without any reference to grammar at all.

A box *of beautiful flowers* were brought by the postman.

I don't like those sort *of sweets*.

My mother came to meet *my sister and* I.

Me *and my friend* went to Greenwich Park.

They saw we *two* crossing the street.

The policeman arrested the man whom *he thought* was guilty.

Other examples will readily occur to the reader. They show the value of utilizing to the utmost the correct forms with which the pupil's mind is already equipped; they suggest the importance of increasing his store of correct forms through the reading of good books. To read much is, in this regard, as necessary as to read carefully. Moreover, we must often do what we now very rarely do—we must give the pupil an opportunity of correcting himself. How many of us are content to leave our writings as they flow from the pen? Do we not revise them again and again? Yet we expect our young children to write clear and accurate English *du premier coup*. We ascribe our own errors to inadvertence, our children's to bad grammar. Instead of having fewer opportunities for revision than the adult, the child should have more. He should have a good chance of finding out for himself if anything is wrong, and, if it is, of rectifying it. The habit of self-criticism thus engendered should precede grammar. It is easier than grammar and more useful.

To secure correct speech the teacher is therefore well advised to place his trust mainly in a generous environment of pure English. When the child is very young, and consequently very impressionable, the mere fact that he forms part of a correct-speaking social group is in itself sufficient to secure reasonably good English. The barbarous English of the child of two causes no alarm : we know that with decent companionship he will gradually shed his linguistic errors and bring about a closer and closer adaptation of his speech to his social models. There is no need for a special corrective. It is only when his models are bad, when he has acquired in the home or the street an inveterate habit of ungrammatical speech, that special correction is called for. And this should take the form of abundant practice in the right usage. For as " one fire burns not another burning," so will a good habit, if sufficiently repeated, supplant a bad one. And here, as elsewhere, individual attention is necessary to success. Each particular child's solecisms should be catalogued by the teacher, just as his diseases are recorded by the doctor. And the effect of the remedies applied should be noted in the one case as in the other. If this had been systematically done in the past, the teacher's faith in the efficacy of grammar would have gone the way of the physician's faith in mediæval drugging.

CHAPTER VII

THE LIMITATIONS OF GRAMMAR (*continued*)

(g) *Analysis and Synthesis*

THE systematic study of the mother tongue, even though no other language be learnt, needs no defence. The informal methods already described are excellent propædeutics to the study of grammar proper, but they are not substitutes for it. They break down at crucial points. They fail to secure that precision in the use of language which clear thinking demands. They afford no principles by which we may criticize the speech of the masses—may judge its consistency with itself and its consonance with the custom of the past. If we trust to the ear only, we have no means of weighing the rival claims of " It is me " and " It is I," of " different to " and " different from," and of many other alternatives where the speech of the common people is at variance with the language of books. Some accident of schooling, too, may have vitiated our standards. " Casabianca," for instance, has been for so long a favourite poem in the classroom, and so freely have we accepted the line "Whence all but he had fled," that its bad grammar has probably escaped our notice. The consequence is a liability to misuse the prepositional "but."

Having decided to teach grammar systematically, we must select the body of doctrine that is to constitute our system. For grammar, however conceived, is a wide and elusive subject. Its content has shifted and changed throughout the ages and its boundaries have always been vague. The Ars Grammatica of the Romans is a very different thing from the Orthography, Etymology, Syntax, and Prosody of Lindley Murray; and much that Lindley Murray thought essential we now regard as extraneous. As treated in the text-book of to-day, the subject is too wide in some respects and too narrow in others. It is too wide inasmuch as it includes material which obviously belongs to other and more abstruse branches of study, such as the distinction—a metaphysical distinction really—between abstract and concrete nouns. It is too narrow inasmuch as it excludes the conditions of lucidity of style as distinct from formal accuracy.

If a boy says, "Tom is much bigger than me," he is lucid without being grammatical; but if he says, "Tom likes me better than Harry," he is grammatical without being lucid.

And who will say that the former fault is worse than the latter? Indeed, the early stages of grammar, formal as well as informal, should be designed to foster a vigilant and critical attitude towards one's own speech. It should include everything that makes for the using of clear, pure, and accurate English.

It is sometimes asked whether the teaching of formal grammar should begin with facts common to all languages, or with facts incidental to one language—with universal grammar, or with specific grammar. This is one of those questions which to the practical teacher have little or no meaning. For he cannot teach universal grammar *in vacuo*; he can teach it only as it is embodied in some particular tongue; and he cannot teach the grammar of any one language without at the same time teaching the principles of universal grammar. The real question is, in fact, one of proportion, not of precedence: which part of the grammar of any language that is being studied deserves the greater emphasis, the part that is peculiar to itself, or the part that is common to all languages? Clearly the latter is more important; it facilitates the learning of other tongues, suggests more basal and elemental problems, and touches a deeper and more permanent order of things. And if foreign languages are taught, this common and universal factor can best be isolated and emphasized by teaching the grammar of at least two languages at the same time.

In studying the structure of language we may begin with the parts of speech or we may begin with the sentence. The older method was to begin with the parts of speech; the newer method is to begin with the unit of speech. And the unit of speech is the sentence.

Starting with the sentence, we analyze it into its two fundamental parts, subject and predicate. The subject-predicate relation strikes deeper than all other grammatical relations. Its roots are to be found in the structure of the mind itself. It is not merely a grammatical form, but a logical and a psychological form as well. Thinking always runs into that particular mould. It is the way our thoughts march forward, and is the explanation of the fact that discourse is broken up into sentences. To quote Professor Stout, " Sentences are in the process of thinking what steps are in the process of walking. The foot on which the weight of the body rests corresponds to the subject. The foot which is moved forward in order to occupy new ground corresponds to the predicate." This is a law which is independent of race or nationality, and there is much to be said for stimulating the young child early in his career to get the " feel "

E

of the sentence and be able to break it up into its two essential constituents.

It has often been suggested that in carrying out this simple analysis the pupil should inquire what engaged the attention of the mind before the sentence was framed. The reply is said to give the subject of the sentence. But does it? Let us test a few cases. When I say, " I saw a big fire in the city yesterday," it is certainly not myself that first occupies my mind. If we take the sentence, " The French defeated the Germans at the Battle of Verdun," and ask a class the proposed question, we are just as likely to get as an answer " the Germans " as " the French," and more likely to get " the Battle of Verdun " than either. As a matter of fact, if this sentence is a genuine expression of thought, it is the-defeating-of-the-Germans-by-the-French-at-the-Battle-of-Verdun that is the real thought-unit, and not any one element that may be discovered therein by reflective thinking. Finally, in making so simple an assertion as " the night was dark," it is really the darkness of the night that first engages the attention, and not the night itself.

We cannot, therefore, lay it down as an in-variable rule that the first thing to do is to search for the subject. The only reason for seeking the subject first is that it is generally

simpler and easier to find. In importance the
predicate is supreme. The simplest pulse of
thought involves a change, and that change is
expressed in the predicate. The subject, regarded from the mental side as distinct from the
verbal, is the indefinite whole within which the
change takes place, with special stress on a particular part which is actually named. This name
is the grammatical subject. Its particularization
is due more to the necessity of communicating
one's thought to others than to the intrinsic
demands of thought itself. At any rate, it gives
little more than a jumping-off ground for that
forward movement of the mind which is the
very essence of thinking. For thinking does not
consist in building up a mental structure by
adding one idea-brick (the predicate) to another
idea-brick (the subject), but rather is it a process
of clearing up bit by bit a vague and indeter-
minate whole. And the clearing up is predica-
tion. In other words, the framing of sentences
is not a synthesis ; nor is composition the opposite
of analysis. There is nothing new in this doctrine :
it is the outcome of a battle settled long ago
in the fields of logic and psychology. The old
associationist or atomic view of thinking has
been definitely abandoned in favour of the
functional view. But discredited doctrines driven
out of other realms of knowledge have a curious

trick of straying into the realm of pedagogy—
much to its detriment.

The heresy that composition is synthesis
derives some support from the etymology of
the word composition. But composition is composition not because thoughts are put together,
but because words are put together. And the
more an essay or story represents the building
of words rather than the marching of thoughts—
the more the words dominate and direct the
thinking—the more wooden and lifeless it appears.
Hence the essential difference between the two
types of composition exercises found in our
schools. One writer laboriously puts together
words that shall mean something, the other
expresses his meaning—presses his thoughts into
forms prescribed by immemorial habits of speech ;
one composes, the other creates ; one writes
because he has to say something, the other
because he has something to say.

It is true that the ways of the reluctant young
composer often give colour to the synthetic
view. He often writes a word or two which
will serve as the subject of a sentence, and then
casts about in his mind for a predicate to fit it.
If this is synthesis, then the synthetic sentence
is a model to be sedulously avoided. For its
vitality is that of a synthetic egg. A real sentence,
on the other hand, expresses a thought that is

born whole. So, indeed, does a good essay, or a good poem, or a good joke. There is a certain organic unity about it which the process of putting it into words searches and reveals, but does not create. "The soul of the poem," says the *Autocrat of the Breakfast-Table*, "is born in an instant in the poet's soul. It comes to him as a thought tangled in the meshes of a few sweet words—words that have loved each other from the cradle of the language, but have never been wedded until now." Some sentences seem to have a strange vitality. They are, as Emerson puts it, vascular and alive : if you cut them they will bleed.

Composition of this virile kind can no more be got by reversing the process of analyzing sentences than a joke can be made by putting together the elements to which humour has been reduced by the metaphysician.

CHAPTER VIII

(h) *Monoglot and Polyglot*

To keep the issue clear and simple I have limited the scope of my arguments to one type of scholar—the monoglot—the child who learns no language but his own. And as at present 90 per cent. of our pupils are allowed to remain monoglot, my conclusions meet the majority of cases.

But the future is big with changes. It is possible that the elementary school boy, with a fair vista of continuation schooling before him, will be required to take up a second language. But whenever a second language is taken it is generally, and wisely, begun quite early. In the past it has been the custom to start French at ten or even earlier; but there has recently grown a tendency to postpone the beginning till the pupil is twelve—a tendency which meets the commendation of the Departmental Committee on Modern Languages, whose Report has recently been published. Does not this fact modify my finding? If the study of formal grammar starts at fourteen and the study of French at twelve, the pupil will have to plunge into French without any previous grammatical preparation. This, however, need not alarm us. If my account of the way in which a command of English is acquired is psychologically sound, the principles laid down will apply with equal fitness to French. It is now indeed universally acknowledged that as far as a living language is concerned (I will deal with dead languages later), the best method of instruction is the direct method. That a little formal grammar helps occasionally is perhaps true ; but the bulk of the work is done by direct and abundant familiarity with the language as spoken and written. Copiousness will in time secure accuracy ; but practice in the mere accurate use of a meagre vocabulary leads to nothing but boredom and ineptitude. It fails to reach even its own very limited objective. When it is considered expedient to teach grammar in the French lesson, the corresponding English grammar may be taught at the same time. That part of English grammar need not be taught before ; it should not be delayed till later. Not only does the English grammar help the French grammar, but the French grammar helps the English. The points of resemblance and contrast elucidate the rules and drive home the instruction. But even so, the amount of grammar that demonstrably expedites the learning of French is surprisingly small.

At present French is taught in those elementary schools only where the pupils are in some way selected. These pupils are either sent as contributions from surrounding schools (as in the case of the central schools), or are selected socially by the fact that the school stands in a good residential neighbourhood. In either case the average intelligence of the children is abnormally high, and grammar might perhaps be begun earlier than in the ordinary school. My own observation, however, indicates that even where children have studied both English and French grammar, as in central schools, for four years, they have so feeble a grasp of its significance —show such impotence in applying their knowledge—that it is doubtful whether the time devoted to it could not be more profitably spent in conversation and in drinking deeper draughts of literature. More matter and less form seems to be needed; more water to swim in and less study of the dynamics of swimming.

Finally, there is the problem of the most fortunate pupil of all—the one who receives a good secondary school education. Can he learn Latin and Greek without grammar ? A few push the direct method so far as to apply it to the dead languages. Others have put forward the theory that when one language is acquired by the natural method—the method by which the mother tongue is acquired—there is no psychological gain in acquiring another in the same way; but there is a distinct gain in translating and composing by the aid of the grammar and the dictionary—in puzzling over knotty passages with no help from either a companion or a crib. There are many who reject this view when applied to a living language, but accept it as applicable to a dead one. The doctrine really amounts to this: the pupil should be put to study Latin and Greek, not to learn Latin and Greek, nor yet to learn what the Latin and Greek writers have to tell us, but in order to gain certain intellectual advantages which accrue from struggling with linguistic difficulties. But the ordinary man, refusing to sacrifice his common sense at the special pleading of the pedagogue, clings to the view that we learn a language in order to understand it. Our ultimate aim is to speak French like a Frenchman, to write Latin like Cicero—or at least to be able to enjoy the literatures of modern France and of ancient Rome. Judged by this standard how do our public school boys stand? How many of them after spending the most educable years of their lives over the study of the classics are able to translate at sight with any degree of facility either Latin or Greek?

How many continue to read these languages in after life for pleasure or profit ? The obvious reply to these well-worn questions points to the conclusion that the grammar way may be a good way to sharpen one's wits on Latin (though even this is very doubtful), but it is not a good way to learn Latin—and we must insist on the plain fact that the object of studying Latin is to learn Latin.

There is a certain sense in which it is manifestly impossible to learn a language without learning its grammar as well, for its grammar is the very essence of its structure. But the term is used in these early chapters in the sense of formal grammar—a systematic study of those uniformities of structure which an examination of a language reveals. And the position is consistently maintained that, whether native or foreign, a language is better learnt through its use than through its grammar ; that although the study of its grammar leads to a greater accuracy in its use, that study can be profitable only when its subject-matter is that part of the language that has already been acquired—that, in fact, grammar is in the main a subsequent and not a prior acquisition. It is of practical value inasmuch as a detection of uniformities in that part of the language which has already been learnt will sometimes make easier the learning of the rest. But use comes first. I hold, in fact, that the direct means is better than the old machinery of rule, vocabulary, and exercise—better even for the classical tongues. This better way was suggested fifty years ago by D'Arcy Thompson in those *Daydreams* of his which have not yet come true—except in such rare places as the Perse Grammar School, where Dr. Rouse's boys begin to learn Latin and Greek by actually speaking them.

To summarize briefly my conclusions, so far as they affect the English pupil: English grammar is of little use in learning English; French grammar is of more use in learning French; Latin grammar is of more use still in learning Latin; but the usefulness of grammar is in every case limited by the fact that it requires a more mature intelligence to grasp the grammar than to learn the language itself, and that for the young mind, instead of making the difficult easy, it makes the easy difficult.

As for a complete and scientific study of grammar, with English as the basal language (a study which an American grammarian describes as "fascinating but useless"), that should undoubtedly be undertaken some time during the student's career. It should be realized, however, that as an abstract science its bearing on the study of literature is but slight. The man of letters is often a poor grammarian. He may be a good philologist, may know much about the pedigree of words, may be familiar with grammatical rules and exceptions ; but as for the logical grounds of classification and definition, the fundamental relation of thought to words and of word to thing, and the universal laws that underlie the expression of meaning—these have little interest for him. For his attitude towards language is in the main sensuous and emotional, rather than coldly intellectual. He loves it for the feelings that it stirs, for the skill with which its web is woven by its master-writers, rather than for those cold and abstract relationships which constitute its grammar. Indeed, the observant teacher will no doubt have discovered that grammatical ability is more closely related to mathematical ability than to linguistic ability.

In dealing with the function of grammar in the teaching of foreign tongues, I speak with diffidence, for the problem is complex and the data upon which to form a judgment are scanty. There is, indeed, an urgent call for experimental work—for a comparison of methods and a rigid measuring of results—for facts and figures rather than theories, for proof rather than opinion. It has been seen from the correspondence that has appeared recently in the columns of *The Times Educational Supplement*, that the grammar problem may be attacked from two distinct quarters.

Professor Sonnenschein and Mr. Watson Bain approach it from the territory of school and college with its traditional doctrines and traditional procedure, Dr. Mercier from the domain of medicine and mind-study. The outlook in one case is that of the pedagogue, in the other that of the psychologist. Without claiming the writers as wholly representative of their class, we may say generally that the pedagogue sets out with the tacit query, How much grammar are we forced to discard? the psychologist with the query, How much grammar are we forced to adopt? The one presents us with a passionate conviction based upon what he calls a long experience in teaching the subject, the other with a dispassionate account of experiments and results. The one is prone to draw his conclusions from the clever child, the other from the average child. As an example of the way in which the newer type of psychologists investigates the grammar problem, I will refer the reader to a book called *Formal English Grammar as a Discipline*, by Dr. T. H. Briggs, published by the Columbia University. It is an elaborate research into the disciplinary effect of grammar : and the conclusion arrived at is that it has no disciplinary effect.

Whether an extraordinarily good teacher might overcome the difficulties which the subject presents to the young, is a question which I have not raised : partly because, although my knowledge of teachers is fairly wide, I have never seen those difficulties overcome ; and partly because the question is not quite relevant. For what we really want to know is what the ordinary teacher can do under the ordinary conditions of school life. More pertinent is the question whether some new method might be discovered which would render this unpalatable subject palatable, this indigestible subject digestible. Doctor Montessori, in her new book on the teaching of children up to eleven, gives much attention to grammar. She describes apparatus which will enable the children to teach themselves. Whether the use of such apparatus would give children a real insight into grammar, or whether it would merely enable them to juggle with words and produce the appearance of knowledge without the reality, I cannot say. It has not yet, I believe, been tried in England : and to condemn a system without a fair trial is contrary to the general spirit of this book. For although my attitude towards the teaching of grammar is sceptical, it is sceptical in the etymological sense only : it regards the question as one to be looked into, to be investigated so carefully that the conclusions meet, as far as possible, the exacting demands of scientific proof.

CHAPTER IX

WATERING-POT AND PRUNING-HOOK

THE young child must speak much before he can speak well; and he must write much before he can write well. Quantity is more important for him than quality; and the English teacher's first concern is with quantity: he must secure a free and copious outpouring of ideas. And everything that checks that outflow is bad, whether it be grumbling or grammar. It follows that the initial attitude of the teacher should be that of encouragement. Directing the attention of his pupils to their successes, he passes over their deficiencies in silence. Not that he is blind to those deficiencies, but that he tries to reduce them by robbing them of interest and energy. He tries, in fact, to starve them out. He so fires his pupils' enthusiasm for merits that the demerits gradually fade away. For there can be no greater blunder than to be always pointing out blunders.

Especially should the teacher refrain from inventing errors for the mere pleasure of rectifying them. He often does invent them with

the recklessness of a doctor inventing diseases.
Having lost formal grammar as a weapon of
attack, he fashions other weapons equally apt to
deaden and stupefy. One of the worst of these
is the embargo he lays on the word *got* when it
indicates possession. Outside the school a remark
such as " I haven't got a watch " would excite no
comment, but within the school it is at once met
with reproof. *Got* used in this sense has become
a solecism and an offence ; and much time (to
say nothing of temper) is spent in getting rid of
it. In a recently published text-book of English
exercises I find whole lessons devoted to the
elimination of *got*. Each child in the class has
to hold an article in his hand while one of them,
acting as interlocutor, stands forth and asks the
same question of each in turn : " James, what
have you in your hand ? " And James gravely
replies, " I have a piece of string in my hand."
A variant form of " Have you seen the muffin
man ? " What happens when the luckless word
got inadvertently slips out, the writer does not
say. Why all this pother about *got ?* What is
wrong with the word ? Its pedigree is beyond
reproach. If the reader will consult the *New
English Dictionary* he will find that Shakespeare
uses the word. So does Swift. Ruskin uses it
frequently, and Augustine Birrell in *Obiter Dicta*
asks, " What has the general public got to do with

literature ? " Johnson in his Dictionary gives possession as a legitimate meaning of the verb *to get*, and quotes George Herbert. Indeed he uses it himself in a letter to Boswell. The only inference we can draw is that it is not a real error, but a counterfeit invented by schoolmasters. Not all teachers, however, shun the word. One of the greatest of them, Edward Thring of Uppingham, whose English is as virile as Swift's, defines a fool as " a person who does not use the sense he has got." What reason then can there be for tabooing a word that has got ingrained in the idiom of the language ? The only pretext seems to be that it is superfluous : there is alleged to be no difference between " I have got a penny " and " I have a penny." I contend there is a difference. The first sentence has more grip in it than the second, and implies a stronger sense of possession. And even if the redundance were proved, it would be insufficient ground for using the pruning-hook. Otherwise we should never be allowed to say that we fall down, for we cannot fall in any other way; nor should we be permitted to say that people meet together, since they can never meet apart ; and our Prayer-book would have to be improved out of all recognition. The truth is that there are many good English phrases which are signs that we are not always content with driving an idea into another

F

person's head : we feel we must sometimes clinch it as well. *Got* is one of our clinching words.

Objections have been raised to *got* even in the sentence, " He got married yesterday " ; whereas every married man knows that the word *got* gives just the right suggestion of capture.

Another stumbling-block to a certain type of academic mind is the conjunction *and*. It is often laid down as a rigid rule that a sentence should never begin with *and*. This was a point on which my own schoolmaster was inflexible. And quite recently a training college student whom I asked to comment on a passage from Malory condemned him for using " the objectionable conjunction *and*." And printers have an ugly trick of emasculating my meaning by turning my periods into commas because they happen to be followed by *and*. Taking down my Bible and opening it at random, I find that the eighth chapter of Exodus contains thirty-two sentences, twenty-five of which begin with *and*. I turn to the first chapter of Sir John Mandeville's *Voyages and Travels*, and find that more than half the sentences begin with *and*. Of the fifth chapter the very first word is *and*. Coming to more modern times, I examine the most beautiful chapter in D'Arcy Thompson's *Daydreams of a Schoolmaster*, the chapter entitled " Place aux Dames," and find that no less than twenty sentences commence with *and*. What, then, can be the objection to this word? When Charles Dickens was the editor of *Household Words* somebody sent him a poem called " A String of Pearls." He returned it with the note : " Too much string." The schoolmaster's disapproval of *and* has a similar origin. He notes that the young scribe is fond of stringing his ideas together with a series of *and's*. And he thinks there is too much string. And there is doubtless good ground for the stricture. But the remedy lies not in destroying the string, but in multiplying and strengthening the ideas—not, at any rate in formulating a rule which is an impeachment of some of the best literature we possess.

The young child, especially the young boy, has a rooted objection to making a laughing-stock of himself : he hesitates to " let himself go." If he loves poetry and poetic expressions he conceals it like a vice. This restraint is not a thing to be buttressed by prohibitions and the cold reception of poetic efforts, but to be worn down by the solvent of approving smiles and encouraging words. When a ten-year-old pupil of mine wrote (I recall the incident through the mist of years) : " The Isle of Man rests on the broad bosom of the Atlantic Ocean," I should indeed have been churlish had I objected to the phrase either on geographical or on æsthetic grounds. It was a phrase to be enjoyed, not dissected and evaluated.

In our slum schools, at any rate, the question of style is so subsidiary as to be almost negligible. Poverty of ideas is the root defect, of which poverty of words is largely, if not entirely, the consequence. Aiming first at exuberance, the wise teacher will postpone cutting and trimming till a later stage; and even then he will do it with a tender hand. In the junior school the watering-pot is more useful than the pruning-hook. What does it matter if the young writer mixes his metaphors a little? We should be grateful that he has metaphors to mix. Let him —if he can—split his infinitives, dislocate his adverbs, detach his participles, and commit all those faults of style which far better people have committed before him. And as for the fine writing to which adolescents are prone, that is a complaint which every boy or girl of parts seems to catch, and, having caught and passed through, is all the better for. At the time he is sincere: the gorgeous phrases fit the prevailing mood. And sincerity in writing outweighs a multitude of defects.

In the year 1897, the year of Queen Victoria's second jubilee, I had to mark the English papers at a certain competitive examination. One of the topics set for the essay was "The Queen's

Jubilee," and I give below the essay written by a candidate named Florence Helen Brace, whose age was fourteen. I later inquired into her past history and found that she was an omnivorous reader : she read anything and everything she could lay her hands on. And she was encouraged by her teachers to express herself with the utmost freedom. Here is the essay :—

"The present is a time calculated to arouse the warmest feelings of loyalty and patriotism in the coldest heart that ever beat in a land governed by our beloved Queen. Sixty years of happiness, peace and safety have rolled by under the sovereignty of the greatest monarch England has ever known ; and now we call aloud to Britain's every son and daughter to celebrate the grand jubilee of love and loyalty. From far-off Australia to mighty India, from rocky Gibraltar to icebound Canada, the glad voices of a million happy subjects come in one great hurrah—a tribute rendered to a reign not only great, but good, not only grand, but noble.

"Never has the throne of Britain been filled by one so loving, so lovely, so truly queenly, and withal so womanly ; so truly queen of home as well as State. Never have childhood, girlhood, and womanhood stood out against the background of history so beautiful and yet so sad. Sorrow has not spared her, Queen Empress as she is ;

Death has come and asked her best-beloved at her hands. Loneliness has come to her, as to so many others, and she has conquered these phantoms with the weapon of prince and peasant alike.

" Alone she stands on her glorious throne, supported as it is by her subjects' love, and wields her sceptre with a sway of gentleness and peace —a sway that, gentle as it is, has done more for England's weal than ever did tyrant's rod of iron.

" During her reign have come the great colonies and dependencies that make our Empire so vast. India, the pearl of the British Crown, Ceylon, the jewel of the Eastern seas, Aden, Gibraltar, Malta, Sierra Leone have all come under Victoria's sway ; and in her reign, too, have lived some of Britain's greatest heroes, greatest poets, greatest writers, and, above all, her greatest women. Then let us reverence the name that will pass from age to age as great, and shout in all loyalty at the great Jubilee day, ' Victoria our Queen ! ' "

I consider this, in spite of its faulty history, a remarkable achievement for a girl of fourteen. I cite it as a sample of what is possible in an atmosphere of encouragement. The writer afterwards took her arts degree at London University, became at an early age the Head Mistress of a school, is a co-opted member of a Local

Education Authority, and takes a prominent part in the feminist movement.

To secure the right atmosphere, we must, among other things, provide incentives : we must see that the writer has a motive for writing. So accustomed are we to lay stress on the fact that speaking and writing are modes of self-expression, that we are prone to overlook the more obvious fact that they are means of communication. And it is the latter fact that affords the motive. The speaker speaks because there is a listener, and the writer writes because there is a reader. No man writes for the mere fun of expressing himself on paper : he addresses himself to some-body whom he wants to influence ; he wants to question him, or inform him, or persuade him, or convince him. He has always at the back of his mind this possible reader or circle of readers —a friend, a côterie, or the world at large. With-out this recipient and responsive factor the business of writing resembles an attempt to work a battery with only one terminal. Whatever else you get, you will get no electricity.

Even when we speak to ourselves, as we, of course, constantly do, for all thinking is a sort of internal speech—even then there is the same duality of speaker and hearer. We speak to an imaginary listener whom we are trying to con-vince that our impulsive acts are really prompted by the highest and most rational motives, or whom we are trying to persuade into our way of thinking on a subject where he is, of course, hopelessly at sea. When any one ponders a thing in his mind, trying to make the matter clear to himself, the " himself " is virtually another person slightly befogged. And it is to be noted that, whatever interpretation we may put on the process, when we do speak to ourselves we are content with a mere adumbration of our meaning. We do not speak in clear and concise terms, with each sentence sharply minted : we are in too much of a hurry for that. Our internal speech is, in fact, fragmentary and not a little chaotic, with a few complete sentences here and there, but the bulk consisting of *disjecta membra*—words and broken phrases and spectral images all mixed up together—and not always actual words, or even the phantoms of words, but often mere blanks which we feel that certain words exactly fit but we cannot stop to find them ; for when we are hot on the scent of a solution, or indeed are merely day-dreaming, we cannot be bothered with reluctant verbiage. To search for the fitting word or the felicitous phrase is a distraction and a nuisance, and when speaking to ourselves the one thing we sedulously avoid is boring ourselves.

When speaking to others, however, this slipshod

thinking will not do : we must exert ourselves to get our meaning clear and complete. The words that suffice for us will not suffice for others. The boy who began his essay on Heroes by saying, "When a man risks another man's life he is called a hero," had, no doubt, an idea in his mind clear enough for himself ; but the reader is liable either to misunderstand him, or to credit him with an insight which he does not possess. Just as the motive for speaking comes from the other person, so does the motive for clearness. And the pains we are willing to take to achieve clearness depends upon our notion of the other person. Mr. Wilfred Whitten, who has recently made some luminous comments on this topic, tells a story of an old editor who tried to teach a young reporter to write clearly. The young man had abilities and ideas, but everything he wrote was confused and opaque, and no amount of advice seemed to do him any good. At last the editor said, "You must really do better. Now, just you take this paragraph back and imagine that you have sitting in front of you the stupidest man in the kingdom ; then tell him, in the simplest and clearest way you can, what you wish to put in the paragraph ; and when you think you have made him understand, write down as clearly as possible what you said to him." The youth went away and soon returned with his revised version. It was a clear and forcible piece of writing. " Capital ! " said the editor. " How did you manage to do it ? " " Well, sir, I did what you told me. I sat down at the desk and fancied you were sitting opposite me." Waiving the undeserved reflexion on the editor's intelligence, I heartily commend the method.

The insufficiency of incentive is signally manifest in the written composition exercises practised in our schools. The pupils are asked to write compositions which are not letters addressed to friends, nor papers to be read to the class, nor articles for the school magazine, nor memoranda for the instruction or entertainment of the teacher, nor writings for any specific purpose or addressed to any specific person. They are just " compositions," and as such are about as inspiring as the remarks made by a man speaking through the telephone with nobody at the other end. It may be urged that the teacher is at the other end. But the teacher rarely has time to read all the essays written by his boys, and when he has he reads them grimly and joylessly. And the pupil knows it. He never tries to amuse the teacher, or to tell him something he did not know before, or to convince him of the error of his ways. Far from wishing to give the teacher pleasure, he directs his energies towards avoiding his anger ; he is content if he just manages to escape a "wigging." He has, in fact, fallen into the school way of imparting knowledge to the knower. In a conversation lesson at an infant school the teacher inquired the number of a cat's feet, the position of his whiskers, and so forth; and a little girl, new to the school, asked in surprise, "Ain't you ever seen a cat, teacher?" She soon, however, got into the school habit of exhibiting knowledge instead of imparting it; or if it be imparting, it is a pouring of water into the sea—which is not a very exhilarating business.

In ordinary life there is a field of common knowledge which we never discuss, merely because it is common knowledge. We never remark that two and two make four, or that a horse's head is at one end of him and his tail at the other. Nor do we unbosom ourselves on the way we spend our Saturdays, or inflict upon our friends vapid sentiments about Spring. But if we discover that under some circumstances two and two make five, we think the matter worth mentioning; and if we have, on a Saturday or any other day, a curious or exciting adventure, we hasten to relate it to our friends. Then there is the wide realm of controversial topics (of politics, morals and social customs, of sport, art and religion), together with the doings of the small world in which we move and the great world in which we intellectually dwell—these are the things that engage our mind. And the things that engage our minds should also be the things that engage our pens. For they are to us the dynamic topics—the topics that strive towards expression —the topics that need but the stimulus of an addressee to flow freely from the pen.

But while the stimulus for written composition is too weak, the stimulus for oral composition is too strong. For the listener in oral composition is a crowd of class-mates, and the task has for the young composer all the terrors and triumphs of public speaking. I do not, of course, refer to the easy-going lesson of the conversational type, but to the more serious and strenuous lesson with older pupils, of whom continuous speech is required. A pupil is suddenly called upon to say something on a theme to which he has recently given no thought. Even supposing he has ideas on the subject, to collect them and arrange them and present them in decent garb is difficult enough at the best of times ; but to have to do these things with teacher and class staring at him and impatiently waiting for him to begin, is an ordeal at which the brightest and bravest may well quail. He wants to succeed ; he longs to succeed. He would love to be able to speak with fire and eloquence to the applause of an admiring class ; but his thoughts are in confusion, and the contrast between his wish and his power fills him with dismay. The stimulus is, in fact, too strong : instead of provoking utterance, it merely provokes stage-fright. The same stimulus, however, with its initial shock tempered by distance and its influence spread over several days, acts as a fine and fruitful incentive. On a recent Monday morning I visited a class of Central school boys about thirteen years of age, and invited twelve of them to deliver to the class on the following Friday afternoon twelve three-minute speeches —one speech each. Each boy was to choose in secret his own topic and make what preparation he thought fit. When the time for testing came they made speeches of which no adult need be ashamed. Some of them were excellent. The list of topics chosen is significant. Here it is: The Unknown Warrior, Modern Improvements, The League of Nations, Wages, Picture Palaces, The Post Office Savings Bank, Prohibition, Capital *versus* Labour, Should Germany be allowed to send goods to England ? Hobbies, Profiteering, and Coal. It will be observed that all these are topics which people do actually speak about both in private and in public. They are vital dynamic subjects, having power in themselves to stir men's thoughts and feelings.

It will be seen, therefore, that to secure the right incentive two things are necessary: a congenial topic and a responsive listener or reader. It is the second factor only that is difficult to find; and then only in written work. As it is, too much strain is put upon the teacher: more responsiveness is demanded of him than one poor soul can supply. The difficulty is partly met by increasing the amount of oral composition and diminishing the amount of written composition. When, however, a child does write, I submit that the product of his pen should be read by somebody (unless indeed it is a mere exercise in reproduction, to which reference will be made later); but that "somebody" need not be the teacher. It may be another pupil, or a friend, or a parent. But whoever the reader is to be, the writer should definitely be told, so that he should know whose mind he is to try to influence. For every vital piece of writing is a deliberate attempt to influence some other human mind.

CHAPTER X

THE IMPORTANCE OF READING

AT first sight composition seems to involve two distinct processes—getting ideas, and putting them into words. And this view is fostered by the obvious fact that there is a relative independence between thought and language. Much thought may be embodied in few words and little thought in many words. Meaning cannot be measured by counting the syllables. To say, " The unfortunate individual was conveyed to his residence in an inebriated condition," sounds as though it ought to mean more than the simple fact that the man was carried home drunk. But it doesn't. There is more sound, but not more sense. When thought and language are happily wedded we get literature—provided, of course, the thought is worthy. But when there is a *mésalliance*, or when one partner unduly dominates, we get a brood of linguistic vices, such as obscurity, jargon, journalese and the Mesopotamia style of oratory. Not that obscurity is always a vice, for language is an expression of emotion as well as of thought, and vagueness is often a potent means of suggesting feelings that are themselves vague, and thoughts that are themselves nebulous and dim. But this impenetrable hinterland of thought is beyond the reach of ordinary prose : it is only the poet who can safely venture within its borders. And there is perhaps something to be said for mere volume of sound in public speaking, if uttered with a due quantum of tears in the voice ; though the judicious are wont to resent it as an attempt to obtain their attention on false pretences. For jargon and journalese there is less defence.

In the mind of the young learner thought and language tend to grow together. Yet sometimes one takes the lead and the other lags behind. When my little girl of four tells me that the fire-engine is going " to un-catch a house on fire," her ideas have outstripped her words ; when she says that " all the little butterflies and burglars have gone to bed," her words have outstripped her ideas. The laggard, however, always strives to overtake the leader. Hence ideas, especially if they are vivid, attract to themselves words of some kind ; and words, especially if they are frequently heard, tend to acquire some sort of meaning—not necessarily the right sort. The more important partner is obviously thought. The sentence owes all its unity and coherence to the thought that lies behind it. Thought is its very soul and substance, the reason for its being and the motive for its utterance. So manifest is this that we are wont to talk of clothing our ideas with words. The only objection to this metaphor is that it suggests that the idea is the same before it is clothed as it is after. The truth is, however, that the relationship is more intimate than this. The idea is, in fact, born clothed—inadequately clothed, no doubt, but still clothed; and the most we can do for it is to change, or in some way improve, its garments. But in the very act of doing so we are changing the idea itself. It does not therefore surprise one to find that a certain school of psychologists hold the view that language and thought are but two aspects of the same thing.

Important as it is that the teacher should approach composition from the side of thought—that he should recognize ideas and not words as the informing and directing force—it is none the less necessary that he should give his pupils words, and give them in abundance. And the best way to give them is through reading. It is a well-known fact that the child from a cultured home speaks better and writes better than the child from an uncultured home. He constantly hears good English spoken, he is conversed with intelligently, he has access to books and pictures; in fine, he dwells in an atmosphere eminently favour-

G

able to the cultivation of gracious speech. The boy from a squalid home is exposed to none of these influences. He has neither ideas nor letters. There are some who deny this, who maintain that the boys in the crowded quarters of our big cities are extraordinarily bright—that they have quite as much intelligence as children from good homes, but they show it in different ways. They have, in fact, everything that the others have except language. Unfortunately, however, this theory will not bear investigation. When subjected to any of the various forms of intelligence tests that do not involve the use of language, these children acquit themselves badly. Even in manual ability they are inferior. Indeed in no form of activity, whether it depends on natural endowment or on special training, can the children from neglected homes, taken as a whole, vie with their better-cared-for classmates. How, then, do they gain a reputation for sharpness? Sharpness they admittedly have, but sharpness is not brightness. It is merely mediocre, or less than mediocre, intelligence working in oblique and dubious paths —in " ways that are dark," and in " tricks that are vain." It means special skill acquired in circumventing hunger or in circumventing the police. Sparrows are sharp, and so are criminals. But sparrows are not highly intelligent birds ; nor do criminals rank high in the intellectual scale.

Indeed, it has been clearly demonstrated that an inordinate proportion of them are mentally defective. We must therefore face the unpleasant fact that the bulk of our poor children are sharp merely as sparrows are sharp, and that their teachers have to supply them with ideas as well as words. And ideas, as well as words, are found abundantly in books.

Reading is the best auxiliary to the teaching of composition that the teacher has at his disposal. I will not go so far as to say that wide reading and good composition invariably go together, but I can confidently say that I know of no school— and I know a large number—where the children read much and the composition is weak; nor do I know of a school where the reading is meagre and the composition good. It is important, therefore, that children should acquire at an early age a taste for reading; and the poorer the children, the more important it is. Whatever method a teacher adopts in teaching reading (and I am inclined to agree with Claparède that our modern methods are all so good that it does not much matter which he adopts) his success may be measured by the speed with which he brings his pupils to the point when the printed page grips them—when they will read for the mere pleasure of finding out what the book has to tell them. At that point the victory is won. All the teacher has to do afterwards is to feed that appetite ; and he can do this by giving his children a profusion of little books—simple fairy tales, or animal stories, or such other things as little children love. When is this point reached ? In good neighbourhoods about the age of seven, in poor neighbourhoods about the age of eight.

A great change has taken place within recent years in the way in which reading is treated in the elementary school. In the best of these schools reading has ceased to be a lesson and has become a pursuit. But not all schools have made the change. Forty years ago the reading lesson, from the top of the school to the bottom, took one of two forms : it was either simultaneous or individual. In the simultaneous lesson the children read in chorus a chapter from the standard reading book. It is doubtful if they took in the meaning of what they read ; but they made a terrific noise. It was fine lung exercise ; but whether it expanded the mind as well as the chest, I cannot say. In the lowest classes the meaning could not possibly be absorbed, for, as a rule, each word was repeated three times before passing on to the next. Nor was the other type of lesson, the individual type, much better. It consisted in reading in turns : one read while the others listened, with their eyes on their own books. The main difficulty was to get the children to follow. In the lower part of the school, and especially in the infant school, every child had to point with finger or pencil to each word as it fell from the lips of the oral reader ; not so much to steady and fix his own attention, as to afford evidence to the teacher that he was following. Meanwhile the teacher walked round from desk to desk in search of " slackers," seizing here and there a vagrant hand and bringing it back with a jerk to the lost place. And to get all the little hands to follow without break the jolting sequence of words, was as arduous a task as to control an armful of squirrels. And no wonder ! Since the object of the lesson was to give practice in reading, every child had his turn, and as the bad readers took twice as long as the good readers to cover the same ground, the bulk of the time was taken up in listening to bad reading—to the halting spelling-out of sounds and syllables. Meanwhile the really good readers were burning to get on with the story and the bad readers were burning to get on with something else. The result was a cumulating boredom and a steady damping-down of any enthusiasm for reading that any of the children might have happened to possess. At the top of the school the scheme was just as bad. There the pupils had often reached a degree of self-consciousness which made reading aloud a trying ordeal—especially if the passage was unprepared. And it always was unprepared. And rarely did the reader read so well that it was pleasanter to listen to him than to read the passage silently. In fact, nobody liked the lesson—neither the teacher, nor the class, nor the individual reader.

Of these two modes of conducting a reading lesson—the simultaneous and the individual—the former has virtually disappeared, but the latter remains to the present day as the staple and standard form of reading lesson in our schools. It is the form affected by most of the old teachers and most of the young. They look with suspicion on silent reading; they say that the children cannot be trusted to read by themselves, and further assert that when they do read by themselves they get no benefit from it. There can be no better reply than to point to the schools (their number is rapidly increasing) that rely for literary culture upon silent reading by the scholars, supplemented by inspiring talks by the teacher, finding as they do that they thus reap a more bountiful harvest than they secured by the older method. After the mechanical art of reading is acquired—and this should never take more than two years—the reading lesson in these schools takes two distinct forms, as in days gone by. But between the old and the new there is a world of difference. The simultaneous reading is replaced by silent reading, and the individual reading, unprepared and deadening, is replaced by an individual reading which is privately rehearsed and publicly inspiriting. For the plan by which the worst readers bore the class has given way to a plan by which the best readers arrest its attention and kindle its imagination. For nobody is allowed to read to the class unless he can do it well, so well that the children gain more than if they read by themselves. And nobody can do it well unless he has familiarized himself with the piece beforehand. The teacher himself frequently reads aloud to the class, treating it with the consideration due to a public audience, and knowing that if he fails to maintain its attention he is himself at fault. So long as his pupils are listening and taking in what he reads, it does not in the least matter whether they are looking at their books or looking at him. Instead of a restraining and repressing force in the reading lesson, he becomes a kindling and quickening influence, appealing indirectly, but none the less powerfully, to the pupils' native impulse to imitate what they admire. And when the thing is done well, everybody enjoys it. The reading is a joy and the listening a delight. The main count in my indictment of the current practice—reading in turns—is that it defeats the very purpose which the reading lesson is intended to fulfil. By making reading a dull and deadly business it creates an active distaste for books.

The lesson itself is only kept going by the application of much driving power by the teacher; whereas the ideal reading lesson should lure and impel by its own intrinsic charm.

The complaint, however, is frequently made that the silent reading lesson fails to impel by its own intrinsic charm : the teacher has to add a little impulsion of his own.   And this is undoubtedly true—sometimes. When it is true it is invariably traceable to the fact that the books are above the children's heads. It is found that Standard IV readers, for instance, are, as a general rule, too hard for Standard IV ; but if these same children are given Standard II readers, they will read them with avidity. The rungs in the school ladder that leads from easy reading to difficult reading are too few and too far apart, especially towards the bottom of the ladder—a defect that is being largely remedied in London by a system of circulating readers. Although I advocate the more generous supply of easy books, I would by no means exclude the highest and best literature on the plea that it is difficult : such literature should have a place of honour in every curriculum. But it is rarely suitable for unaided study. Its merits—especially its shyer merits—are not apparent at first blush : they must be discovered and disclosed by the teacher. In fact in the literature lesson proper the pupils must be led to read for themselves rather than left to read for themselves.

How are we to regard the penny dreadful ? Is it a friend of the school, or an enemy ? There was a time when magistrates were wont to ascribe every youthful lapse from rectitude to the cheap novelette. Nowadays it is the cinema that gets the blame. It is true that the penny dreadful has lost much of its blood and some of its thunder. The open and flagrant wickedness of Dick Turpin, Deadwood Dick, Jack Harkaway, Spring-Heeled Jack the Terror of the Antilles, and Sweeny Todd the Demon Barber of Fleet Street—heroes who moved the minds of past generations of boyhood —the open wickedness of these has passed into obscurity. Their very names sound strange to the modern schoolboy. No longer are their titles flaunted side by side with the *Police News* and other pink publications in those curious little shops in the back streets of London that sell the baser sort of literature. In their place we find periodicals that record the doings of Sexton Blake, Nelson Lee, Tubby Haig, Buffalo Bill, and Robin Hood. These tales fall into five groups according as they deal with Cowboys, Football, School Life, Medieval Adventure, or the Detection of Crime. And when they deal with two at once, as in the Nelson Lee series (Nelson Lee is both a schoolmaster and a detective), the high-water mark of popularity seems to be reached.

The school stories differ from the older type in being on the side of law and order : they do not hold the masters up to ridicule, nor do they glorify insubordination and the breaking of rules. If a master figures as a fool, he is exceptional ; and if he is baited and hoaxed, it is not because he is a master, but because he is a fool. The author tries to secure verisimilitude by a free use of schoolboy slang. At St. Frank's, the school of Nelson Lee and Nipper, " giddy " is the great word. Everybody is giddy. Even inanimate things suffer from the general vertigo. " He won't open his giddy mouth " ; " Dick acts the giddy ox generally " ; " the bits of furniture we see in any giddy study " ; " his father is shoved in the giddy county court for debt " ; " a giddy fine thing—I don't think " —all these are extracted from the same story, a story which, on the whole, is fairly well written. St. Frank's, in common with its rivals, is eminently " classy " : it enrols among its scholars the Duke of Somerton, the Hon. Douglas Singleton, and Sir Montie Tregellis-West.

The detective stories are palpable imitations of Conan Doyle, with Sherlock Holmes in the thinnest of disguises tracking down criminals with a sagacity that never fails. The great detective's tricks of manner and method are shamelessly copied ; and even his place of residence. Sexton Blake has rooms in Baker Street, and Nelson Lee, although the house-master at a school, has rooms in Gray's Inn Road.

The Cowboy and Indian stories, the invariable hero of which at the present time is Buffalo Bill, have a distinct style of their own. The one story from which I shall quote starts off thus : "A thoughtful frown corrugated Buffalo Bill's brow as he stood at the door of his private car." A band of Indians are described as "fierce and feathered figures mad with torture-lust." Into these wild parts enters Montelier, the Gentleman Desperado, "a man who walked with a dainty, sinuous, almost feminine, grace ; a man who held a shining monocle in one eye." "The prince of desperadoes made an elaborate gesture with a rosy, bejewelled hand," and "very deliberately flickered his nose with a dainty silk handkerchief." The common writer of sensational stories is content to make his hero appear on the scene the moment before the innocent man is shot. The finger is on the trigger, but the gun is not fired. The writer of this story goes one better : he brings the rescue still nearer the verge of the disaster. Buffalo Bill arrives too late to prevent the tomahawk being flung at his friend, who is tied to a tree, but he fires at the flying weapon, and "then the tomahawk seemed to buck and jolt in its flight, seemed to split in two, then went hurtling and spinning to the ground." This is not so much stretching the arm of coincidence as pulling its leg.

Speaking generally, the boys' papers of to-day are always full of adventure, are often blood-curdling, and are sometimes silly. But they are never immoral. They are never immoral in the sense of confusing the categories of right and wrong, or of making evil more attractive than good. Crime is always punished; virtue is always rewarded. They are, in fact, as inveterately moral as melodrama. Even Robin Hood's mis-deeds (the medieval hero of the hour is Robin Hood) shine by contrast with the misdeeds of his enemies. He is more virtuous than the respect-able citizens, and has as much goodness in him as an outlaw possibly could have.

As for girls' papers, nothing could exceed their scrupulous propriety. So far as I can judge from the one periodical that every schoolgirl seems to read, the prim attitude of the maiden aunt is never departed from. This particular journal deals week by week with the doings of the girls at Cliff House, a boarding-school of high repute, where the mistresses are models of rectitude, and all that is lady-like and proper is fostered by the tone, the general atmosphere, and the sympathy between teacher and taught. The bulk of the girls are always on the side of authority. The rebellious get no encouragement from their classmates; the good meet with their universal approval.

It is difficult at first sight to see how adventure and fun can be got from a community so virtuous and dull. But they are got in inexhaustible quantities. The stories of the school seem endless. The tap is turned on every Thursday, and a given measure of narrative is doled out to a crowd of eager customers. Each story is a crude comedy of manners. There is the rich girl who " swanks," and the poor girl who tries to hide her poverty; the noble girl who suffers in silence rather than implicate some other girl base enough to accept her sacrifice; the mysterious girl who has some secret sorrow feeding on her damask cheek—and above all there is Bessie Bunter. Bessie is perennial. She gives continuity to the tales. The other characters shift and change from week to week: now one is the centre of interest, now another; new girls enter the school and old girls leave; the seasons roll by and the terms pass into years. But Bessie Bunter remains unchanged. Amid a world of variables she alone is constant. Shakespeare foreshadowed her in the fat knight who swaggers through his plays. Bessie, too, is fat and swaggering, and she loves good living; but she differs from Falstaff in one essential point.

Falstaff claims, and justly claims, that he is not only witty in himself, but the cause that wit is in other men ; while Bessie, although she is undoubtedly the cause that wit is in other girls, cannot by her most generous admirer be called witty. Her goggles, her clumsiness, her greed, her thick skin, her general flatfootedness and stodge, make her the butt of all the other girls. Like the funny man in melodrama, she is put into all the tales to supply the comic element. And there is no doubt about her being comic. The mere mention of her name to a class of schoolgirls—and schoolboys, too, for that matter—is enough to raise a laugh. Bessie Bunter has, in fact, become a household word and a schoolroom joke.

The curious thing is that all this reading is done furtively. The school authorities take no cognisance of it ; the home authorities either connive at it or actively forbid it. And yet it goes on. If you inquire in the lower forms of a secondary school or the higher standards of an elementary school, you will find that nearly every boy has a shocker in his satchel. It will require a little tact to get him to produce it. When you first broach the matter you arouse his suspicions : he will put on a surprised look, as though he had no idea what you were talking about. But in the gentle warmth of a smile and a joke, and a sly hint that you have a secret liking for thrillers yourself, he will grow expansive and bring forth his treasure. It is significant that a fondness for these sensational stories is almost universal among children whose ages range within two or three years each side of thirteen; and the more intellectual the child, the greater, as a rule, is the avidity with which he reads them.

If we object to these stories at all, it seems to me that we can only do so on æsthetic grounds. It is their literary craftsmanship that is bad, not their moral influence. Indeed I know of no penny dreadful quite so perversive of common honesty as Raffles; and no cheap school-tale quite so prejudicial to school discipline as Stalkey and Co. Mr. G. K. Chesterton, in an essay called "A Defence of Penny Dreadfuls," writes thus: "Among these stories there are a certain number which deal sympathetically with the adventures of robbers, outlaws and pirates, which present in a dignified and romantic light thieves and murderers, like Dick Turpin and Claude Duval. That is to say, they do precisely the same thing as Scott's *Ivanhoe*, Scott's *Rob Roy*, Scott's *Lady of the Lake*, Byron's *Corsair*, Wordsworth's *Rob Roy's Grave*, Stevenson's *Macaire*, Mr. Max Pemberton's *Iron Pirate*, and a thousand more works distributed systematically as prizes and Christmas presents. Nobody imagines that an admiration of Locksley in *Ivanhoe* will lead a boy to shoot Japanese arrows at the deer in Richmond Park; no one thinks that the incautious opening of Wordsworth at the poem on Rob Roy will set him up for life as a blackmailer."

And again: "It is the modern literature of the educated, not of the uneducated, which is avowedly and aggressively criminal. Books recommending profligacy and pessimism, at which the high-souled errand-boy would shudder, lie upon all our drawing-room tables." Perverse and paradoxical as Mr. Chesterton often is, here he is talking plain common sense. The plea that our books are literature, while the errand-boy's books are not, will not serve. In fact it merely aggravates the offence. For if there is anything in Miss Mason's theory that text-books fail to teach because they are badly written, and that knowledge if put into literary form slips easily into the mind and stays there, then the influence of a bad good book, if I may so put it, is more pernicious than the influence of a bad bad book.

It is, I repeat, the literary craftsmanship that is bad, and not the moral influence. And when I come to look more closely at it, I am not so sure about the badness of the craftsmanship. It requires no small amount of artifice to write stuff that grips the attention of the young as these tales do. That they do not represent life as it is, is a criticism that may be urged against many an acknowledged classic. Indeed the very fact that they keep life at a respectful distance reduces the chance of their influencing conduct by inciting the reader to imitation. And as for the quality of the English, it is no better and no worse than that of half the books that stand on the shelves of the school library. The ordinary adult, at any rate, who will devour the vapid and silly stories of the bookstall magazines has no right to scoff at the cheap novelette. His own stories are better printed and better illustrated, that is all.

There is matter here for both the schoolmaster and the publisher to ponder. I personally hold the view that this surreptitious reading is, on the whole, a benefit to the school; not because it is surreptitious, but because it is reading. It makes the child familiar with words and the printed page; it extends his vocabulary and gives him a sense of syntactical structure. In fine it is a form of literary education. It is true that both subject-matter and treatment are often regrettably poor; but it is the business of the schoolmaster to wean his pupil from the trashier sort of novelette and lead him to something better. This cannot be done by ignoring the novelette, nor yet by telling the pupil that there is no real pleasure to be got from reading it. One might just as well try to get him to give up toffee by telling him that toffee is not sweet. We must start with the novelette

H

end of the scale of values, and not with that higher end which is far beyond his mental reach.

It is the business of the publisher to find out if he can import into his school readers some of the attractive—legitimately attractive—elements of the novelette. It is clear that humour is one of these elements. The glaring lack of humour in official school books is a fact that has often been pointed out by Mr. E. J. Kenny.

There is yet another point of view which the culture-epoch theorists are wont to stress. It is that children in their early teens are passing through that stage of development which corresponds with the hunting and most adventurous period of racial history. And in these thrilling stories certain deep-rooted impulses find a healthy vent. The old doctrine of Catharsis applies : the bosom is cleansed of much perilous stuff that stirs within the heart. The intelligent youth goes through the process and comes out the other end. It is a tenable theory that those who read rubbish when they are old are those who did not read rubbish when they were young.

CHAPTER XI

THE MAKING OF SPEAKERS

To the last generation of teachers oral composition as a school subject was unknown ; teachers of the present day know it well enough, but know not what to do with it. They realize its importance, they recognize it as essential to the proper training of a child ; but it baffles and perplexes them. Rarely do they feel that they are getting full value out of the lesson. The mode of attack is tentative and uncertain, varying from school to school and from class to class. And certain opinions have sprung up which increase the confusion and tend to obscure and defeat what I regard as the vital aim of oral composition. These heretical opinions are four in number : that oral composition is easier than written ; that it has no separate *locus standi* of its own, but is a mere handmaid to written English ; that it requires no preparation on the part of the pupils ; and that it is gradually to be supplanted by written composition as the pupil proceeds up the school.

Let me at once lay it down as a dogma that *the function of the oral composition lesson is to train for public speaking and public debate.* If this is not its sole function, it is at least its main function. It is its distinguishing mark, its patent of nobility, its warrant for admission into the circle of school studies. If it does not mean practice in public speaking, but merely practice in polite conversation, or a verbal give and take between teacher and class (as so many oral composition lessons virtually become), it has no justification for appearing in the time-table at all; for every oral lesson is in this sense an oral composition lesson. And the framing of simple isolated sentences, whether written or oral, cannot properly be called composition. A child is not composing in any profitable sense unless he develops a theme. To compose orally is to speak continuously and connectedly to an audience—whether it is an audience of one or a thousand. There are, of course, occasions when oral composition is easier than written. A child of six, for instance, can tell a story better than he can write it. But that is because he cannot write. Once the mechanical art of writing and spelling is mastered, oral composition is much the more difficult. It demands a more concentrated effort of attention and involves a greater nervous strain.

Speaking differs from writing in many of its features. There is a certain pace at which ideas can pass comfortably through the mind—a pace at which interest is fed and attention is not fatigued—a pace which, within certain limits, varies with the individual. The reader of a book can choose his own speed : the hearer of a discourse has his forced upon him. And as there is for the listener no stopping and going back to pick up a lost thread of meaning, the speaker has to see to it that the thread is not easily lost. On the platform repetition is not only allowable, but desirable ; and sentences that would be condemned as ambiguous if they appeared in print, become clear as crystal when spoken with the right emphasis. Oratory is looser in texture than prose, as well as more repetitive in pattern. The ideas are attenuated and diluted in order to be the more readily absorbed. Speaking is more plastic, too, more sensitive to response. "Writing," says Oliver Wendell Holmes, "is like shooting with a rifle ; you may hit your reader's mind or miss it ; —but talking is like playing at a mark with the pipe of an engine ; if it is within reach and you have time enough, you can't help hitting it." A careful investigation has revealed marked differences in the type and prevalence of errors in the two forms of composition. Certain types are more frequent in oral composition, others in written. It follows from all this that a good speech and a good essay are two distinct things : they overlap, but do not coincide.

The oral composition lesson commonly heard in our schools has all the defects of reading in turns, with a few special ones of its own. The teacher is taking a class, say, of Standard IV boys. He writes on the blackboard the heading, *A TRAMCAR*, and invites his boys to give him a sentence about it. They are by no means eager to unbosom themselves on the subject of tramcars, and it requires a little pressing to get them to start. At last one ventures with, "A tramcar goes on tram-lines." Another offers, "A tramcar is full of people." After a few suggestions of this kind have been made, the teacher selects, modifies, or combines one or two statements, and down goes the first sentence on the blackboard. Then he asks for more, and the game of pumping for platitudes drags wearily on for about half an hour, at the end of which time something of this kind appears on the blackboard:

A TRAMCAR

A tramcar is a large vehicle which runs on rails. It used to be drawn by horses, but is now generally driven by electricity. It carries people inside and outside. The man who stands at the front of the car is called the driver, and the man who gives out tickets is called the conductor. When a passenger wants the car to stop he pulls a bell.

Many would regard this as a successful lesson of its kind. Wherein does its success consist? The boys learn one new word (vehicle), and one new fact (that trams used to be drawn by horses), both supplied by the teacher. Their feeling for pronunciation, too, especially for the placing of the full stop, is perhaps made a little more acute. That is about all. As against this slight gain, let us consider what has been missed. In the first place, practice in oral composition has been missed. The statements offered by the boys were little more than mere ejaculations : they were certainly not continuous discourse. Nor were they made by the same boy. The only composer or putter-together was the teacher, and even he merely achieved that patchwork form of writing which differs *toto cœlo* from the dynamic or creative form—the only form really worth cultivating.

The second thing missed was the joy of work. Nobody liked the lesson—neither the insistent teacher nor the reluctant scholars.

Let us contrast with this lesson two other attempts to deal with the same, or a similar, topic. The first was at a girls' school, where a pupil of thirteen stood before her class and spoke continuously for three or four minutes about an omnibus, a subject she had herself chosen. She did not waste time and kill interest by telling the girls, some of whom had come to school by omnibus, that an omnibus runs on wheels, or that the conductor wears uniform and punches tickets; but she talked as though she were trying to amuse the family circle; she related a little incident she had witnessed in an omnibus. It was about a finical and captious old lady who entered the 'bus with a number of small parcels, and had much difficulty in getting at her money to pay her three-halfpenny fare; and when she did get at it she found that she had nothing less than half-a-crown; and after she had handed it to the conductor and he had counted out the change, she discovered that there were three half-pennies at the bottom of her bag after all; and she insisted on the conductor giving her back her half-crown. What the conductor said, and what the old lady said, and especially what she further said when she found that she had been carried past her destination, were related with much gusto and with no small sense of humour. Everybody listened and everybody laughed and everybody enjoyed it. But she did not do this on the spur of the moment: she had had a week to think about it.

Another example, better still. A boys' school this time, and a central school. There I heard a lad of fourteen speak for an hour about a tramcar, illustrating his discourse with numerous drawings and diagrams and models. Some of the drawings were made at the time on the blackboard, others had previously been prepared on large sheets of paper. All were designed to explain and illustrate the principles underlying electric traction. The boy showed how the electricity is generated at the power station, how it is conveyed to the tramcar, and how it makes the tramcar move. It was, in fact, a good scientific lecture. And the class listened with absorbed attention. So did I. And this, mark you, is not an isolated achievement. It was only a week before that I listened in the same classroom to an even better lecture. The subject that time was a steam engine. There are other boys in the class who are willing, nay, eager, to undertake similar tasks—tasks which involve long and careful preparation. There must, you think, be some fire in the teaching that can do this. True ; but the fire does not all come direct from the teacher. Some of it comes from the method, which is itself full of stimulus and incentive.

I regard it therefore as a maxim of cardinal importance, that *oral composition should always be prepared.* For it is in the preparation that its cultural value lies. The public utterance is not the growing process, but rather the final flower and reward. Even if it were not so, even if the faltering efforts of the pupil forced against his will to speak extempore did have some disciplinary effect upon his mental powers, it would by no means compensate for the depressing effect upon the class. Even adults with a wide range of knowledge and experience seldom speak well at a moment's notice. The best impromptu speeches are, I am told, very carefully prepared. To impose on the immature mind a task that is beyond the powers of the mature mind, is to court certain failure.

It is surprising what keenness is displayed in an oral composition lesson where chosen members of the class are due to deliver little prepared speeches, especially if the non-speakers are required to vote by ballot for the best speeches. Some of the speakers write out their speeches and learn them off by heart; but this does not produce the best effect: it savours too strongly of reciting. The first little speech I listened to was of this sort. Here it is:

THE UNKNOWN WARRIOR

Boys of Class V, I am now about to deliver a short speech on the man who won the war, or the Unknown Warrior.

Amidst the most solemn ceremonies and with the most loving care, he who henceforth is to have a resemblance (?) of the heroic qualities of the British race, has received his place in the midst of the departed great. The Unknown Warrior, taken from the bosom of the battlefield where his blood won the victory, has been laid to rest in Westminster Abbey.

There he will sleep, surrounded by the royal and the noble who have for centuries past made the history of England. Close by lie the men who in their time have won the favour of their countrymen, either in art or in literature. Famous generals are gathered there, whose names will always leap into the minds of people who think of the gallant things Englishmen have done in times past. In the midst of all these, in future will be seen the tomb of the Unknown Warrior who has been laid to rest amongst so many great men. Yet he comes from the lowest ranks of the British Army.

He is called the Unknown Warrior, but he is only unknown in name, for we all know that he is the worthy son of the British race who has so gallantly laid down his life for King and country.

Now, my friends, I am sure you will all agree with me when I say that the Unknown Warrior deserves all the honour and glory the country has bestowed on him. I trust that by next year we shall have a monument erected in memory of all those brave sailors who lost their lives at sea while defending Britain's shores.

The speaker, who was very small for his age (thirteen), rattled off this speech at great speed. The contrast between his size and his language gave one the impression that he was wielding far too heavy an instrument, and suggested that somebody else had written the speech and he had learnt it off by heart. The speech, however, was undoubtedly his own : it was of a piece with other things he had written at the school.

The sort of advice it is well to dole out to beginners—in discreet doses, at opportune moments, and in language modified to suit this age—is something like this : Put your trust in ideas, not in words. The vital thing is to have something to say which is worth saying. If you write out your speech, don't try to learn the words. The only two sentences it is always wise to get by heart are the first and the last ; the first enables you to start with confidence, the last gives you the feeling that you can, when you want to, finish off neatly. It sometimes happens that the piquancy of a remark, or the point of a joke, depends on a particular phrase : remember that phrase word for word. For the rest, meditate your speech, but don't memorize it—except, of course, the leading ideas. Get those clear, and settle in your mind their most appropriate sequence. Getting the ideas clear often means talking to yourself about them, expressing them mentally in a variety of forms. Some of these forms will strike you as being more felicitous than others; these will probably stick in your mind and be ready for use when you need them. When you are on your legs, let yourself go. Forget yourself, forget your manuscript, if you have one—forget everything except your ideas. Bend all your efforts towards communicating those ideas clearly and vividly to your audience. The words will, as a rule, look after themselves—if you have previously pondered your subject-matter. They will come readily. Even if they come tardily, it does not matter. So long as you are hot in the pursuit of a project, your audience will gladly follow you, and an obstructing hurdle here and there will only add zest to the chase. A reluctant word is a mere nothing; a reluctant thought is more serious. For the ideas are the life and soul of your speech. Let them live and breathe through your words; don't choke them with verbiage. In a story the ideas are the events, and their sequence is fixed for you; all you have to do is to memorize that sequence.

In a controversial subject (Prohibition, for instance) you have to make a sequence as well as memorize it. And the links between the ideas are not so strong and certain as in a chain of events. Many speakers find it necessary to have notes, each leading idea being represented by a key-word or a key-phrase. The use of notes is threefold : they give you confidence ; you can consult them if you are gravelled ; and you can assure yourself at the close that you have not left out anything of importance. Do without notes if you can ; if you cannot, use them as little as possible.

Beware of purple patches. If they make the rest of your speech look mean and shabby, cut them out ruthlessly. If you have a short time to speak, don't make it shorter by telling the audience that your time is short : they know that as well as you. Don't start with irrelevant personal confidences ; nobody wants to know what you felt like when you were first asked to speak : what they want to know is how you are going to acquit yourself now. In fact, avoid introductions altogether : dive straight off into your subject.

You will feel nervous at first ; but with practice in speaking that will wear off. You must struggle to get rid of self-consciousness. The only way to stop thinking about yourself is to think hard about something else—to give full scope to your desire to give pleasure to your audience. Part of your nervousness is due to your fear of making a fool of yourself. That fear is itself foolish. Everybody makes a fool of himself sometimes— unless he happens to be a fool always. To fear being laughed at is a form of conceit ; and to be conceited is a much worse fault than to be a bad public speaker.

Advice of this kind will be helpful mainly to pupils at continuation schools, and to older children generally ; but some of it will suit the younger children. It is not suggested that all oral composition lessons should take the form suggested above : there are other forms which, whether they are as good or not, should be practised for the sake of variety. Debates, for instance, and certain kinds of dramatization. As these, however, are widely known, I will merely remark that the participants should always be given ample time to think about what they have undertaken to do.

A favourite form of oral exercise consists in describing a picture. It virtually means telling in a disjointed and haphazard way what is seen in the picture. The exercise can, however, be made a severe test of a pupil's descriptive powers. Let him take a picture which the rest of the class have not seen, and describe it to them as systematically and as completely as he can. Then let each child make a drawing, plain or coloured, of what he thinks the picture looks like. By comparing these drawings with the original, the speaker will realize how far he has succeeded (it will not be far) and in what respects he has failed.

A novel and suggestive view of composition has recently been put forward by Mrs. Douglas Truman, in her book *The Child Vision*. To her, composition is a unique means of mental training, as it affords the one easy and natural passage from concrete thinking to abstract thinking. What life's hurly-burly does slowly and badly, composition does quickly and well. Mrs. Truman's starting-point is neither things nor words, but mental pictures. She, of course, insists on the importance of primary experience—of direct contact with reality—but composition begins with that experience as it appears in the child's visual imagery. Hence the title of her book. The beginner describes orally to the class a picture he sees in his mind, and the class proceeds to draw it. These drawings serve as a criticism of the description. But this is only the starting-point. The theory put forward is that we begin by thinking in images (assumed to be mainly, if not entirely, visual images); we pass on to thinking in words; and we finally learn to think without the help of either images or words. That we tend, as we get older, to pass from the first stage to the second, there can be little doubt ; that we ever reach the third is open to a great deal of doubt. Be that as it may, Mrs. Truman has developed a systematic method, and, judging from the results she gives, a very successful method, of teaching composition.

The problem of correction is a little more complex in oral than in written work. A child in a poor district generally has two more or less distinct dialects—one which he speaks at school, and another which he speaks in the street, the playground, and the home. It is the latter which is his more natural and spontaneous utterance ; the one he uses when he lets himself go, or is in any way off his guard. The school speech is a more recent and more fugitive acquisition : to maintain it demands constant vigilance on his part. The teacher has to throw the whole weight of his influence and authority into the scale of cultured speech ; he must increase its bulk and magnify its prestige ; he must try to make it more natural for the child to speak the mother tongue than to speak his mother's tongue. In this difficult, but not impossible task reading is perhaps the teacher's most powerful ally. It is true that the book itself does not tell him how to pronounce the words, but it serves to steady

I

his pronunciation and to restore sounds that have become perverted or lost. The boy, for instance, who constantly sees the word *nothing* ending in a *g*, will be unlikely to go on pronouncing it as though it ended in a *k*. When children learn English mainly through the medium of books, as they do in certain parts of Wales, their speech is never slipshod : when it departs from standard English pronunciation it always moves towards a scholarly preciseness, never towards a vernacular carelessness.

As a general maxim of method I suggest the following : *Merits should be exhibited in public, defects in private*. Since it is far more important that thirty-nine pupils should listen to good models of speech than that one should obtain practice in public speaking, it is only the better pupils that should be allowed to perform before the class : the poorer should be heard at the teacher's desk while the others are engaged in something else. The maxim forbids the use of the oral lesson as a rehearsing period for the inefficient ; for rehearsals aim, among other things, at the elimination of errors, and the elimination of errors should be, as far as personal errors are concerned, at any rate, a private affair.

To reduce the need for the individual rectification of errors, the teacher should first ascertain what errors his children actually make. If he will collect, analyze, and classify these errors, he will be surprised to find how few are the rules that actually are broken. In an investigation made in America it was found that 71 per cent. of all oral errors fell under five types, and 91 per cent. of written errors under ten types.[1] Once these common errors have been catalogued, a stubborn attempt should be made to kill them. And the best way to kill them is to starve them out—to dislodge them by firmly establishing in their place the correct forms, which by frequent usage become an organic part of the fibre and structure of the mind.

If this be done, there is little room left for individual correction : the errors peculiar to individual pupils will not be many; and these may be dealt with privately. At any rate, the teacher should rigidly avoid interrupting a pupil's public speech in order to correct a blunder. It is stopping the plough to catch a mouse. It will put the speaker out of his stride, will check the momentum of his speech, will disturb that confidence which is essential to good speaking, and will probably cause him to smart under a sense of not being given a fair chance—a sense of injustice, in fact. All pupils will not perhaps feel like this, but many will; many will find interference as offensive as nagging. Besides,

[1] See Daniel Starch's *Educational Psychology*, pp. 364-5.

correction in the midst of speaking fails of its purpose : if the speaker attends to his blunder he forgets his speech, if he attends to his speech he ignores his correction. Since, however, his blunder was made in public, it should also be rectified in public ; else the hearers might accept it as a correct form of speech. But the rectification should be delayed till the speech is over, and should be made in so kindly a spirit, with so generous an admixture of praise for the merits of the speech, that all sting is taken out of the criticism. Nothing is to be gained by robbing a pupil of his *amour propre*.

CHAPTER XII

THE MAKING OF WRITERS

BEFORE a child can write he must have something to say; and before he can write well he must have something to say that is vital and significant—something that interests himself, gripping his mind and stirring his pulse, or something that he feels to be of interest to the world at large. The ideas to be expressed must be those that he has, or those that he ought to have and can readily acquire. They must, in fact, be either personally important or universally important.

In setting a theme for an essay it is well to offer a choice of subjects, for it rarely happens that one topic suits the whole class. If it belongs to the personal group, such as "How I spent my last Bank Holiday," we cannot be sure that it interests all the scholars: some may have had a dull time and have forgotten all about it, while others may have had so exciting a time that the essay almost writes itself. If the topic belongs to the impersonal group, "Aeroplanes," for example, there is still the difficulty that some of the pupils may know much about it and others nothing; that to some of them the topic is fascinating, to others quite unattractive. At competitive examinations there is often no choice. This is, of course, due to the difficulty of equating essays on different topics : it is hard to estimate, with any pretence at precision, the comparative merits of an essay on "Tadpoles" and an essay on "The Great War."

In the United States they try to get over these and other difficulties by using a standardized Marking Scale, which consists of several pieces of composition arranged in order of merit and carrying definite scores. When an essay is to be valued, it is compared with the samples in the scale, and allotted the same mark as the sample it most closely approximates in merit. Of the many scales in use, the most interesting for our present purpose is the Harvard-Newton scale, for the instructions given for its use point to wide differences in practice between ourselves and our American cousins. The Bureau of Educational Measurements and Standards, Kansas State Normal School, has laid down certain hard and fast conditions under which papers to be assessed by the scale must be written. Two periods of forty minutes each are allowed for the essay—one for collecting facts and writing a rough draft; the other for corrections and for writing out a fair copy. The two periods may occur on the same day, or on different days. During preparation the pupils are permitted to ask the teacher questions and to use an encyclopædia, a dictionary, or any other book of reference; but they may do none of these things after they have started to write. The essay should be about 150 words in length, and must not exceed 200 words. The pupil is given a list of suggested subjects, but his choice is not restricted to this list : he may write on anything, provided he has not written on it recently. The list is of interest from many points of view. Here it is :

Boys

Outdoors : The best way to catch rats. How to build a shelter for the night. The hired man. When I helped father harvest. Should a town boy own a dog? When the horse ran away.

Mechanics : How to run a Ford. Is a Ford better than a Saxon? Our mowing-machine. How to dam the creek. How to make a rabbit trap.

Games : My first baseball game. Should football be abolished? Is —— better than ——? (Fill in the names of two authors of juvenile stories.) Should a boy be made to go to school ? The use of keeping pet rabbits. Is it right to catch fish with a hook ? Should a boy play marbles for keeps ?

Girls

Home : My room. How to get the best breakfast I know. When the lamp tipped over. Which is better in the home, music or art ? Ought boys and girls take piano lessons ?

Social : My new dress. How to eat soup. My first party. When Mr. ———'s house burned. The worst boy I ever knew.

School : When a bird came into the schoolroom. How I killed giant Laziness. Is Latin more useful than science ? The inside of my desk. The boy across from me.

Boys and Girls

When I become a voter. The work I like best. Is a college education worth while ? Teacher.

This list is open to criticism on the ground of both subject-matter and wording. It is hard to understand how people who make much ado about correcting such phrases as " I have got," " He sat by me " (corrected to " *near* me "), " It was me," and sentences which begin with *why, and,* or *so*— all of which expressions are defensible, are indeed used by our greatest writers—it is hard to understand how these same critics can present as models of English : " The boy across from me " (whatever it may mean), and " Ought boys and girls take piano lessons ? "

The scheme, however, points to many weak spots in our own system. To begin with, the American pupils are given time and opportunity to prepare their essays : they are not expected to write straight off out of their heads. Our pupils are. It is true that we often announce to the class some days beforehand what the subject of the coming essay will be, but we give the children no opportunity to collect facts in school ; nor do we ever, under any circumstances, permit them to make a rough draft. To quote what I have said on this matter in *Mental Tests :* " When the pupil has finished his exercise he should be given a chance to revise it. Many of the mistakes which we point out to him he could quite well, with a little trouble, find out for himself. When you or I write anything, rarely do we leave it as it first flowed from the pen. We set it aside and read it again later : we score out superfluous words, change awkward phrases, rearrange the ideas, and sometimes, indeed, write the whole thing over and over again. All careful writers do this. If they do not actually do it on paper, they do it in their heads before committing it to paper. To revise and to remodel, to reflect upon what is written, and to reject even the good in favour of the better—that is at least part of the secret of clear and vigorous prose. We do this ourselves, but we do not allow our pupils to do it. Often do we expect them to write without preparation ; always do we expect them to write without revision. Second thoughts are discouraged ; for erasures are discouraged. The pupil must try to present a fair page of writing without blot or blemish. So chary are the children of crossing anything out, that if they make a mistake in phraseology or in spelling, they enclose the peccant word in brackets and leave it there. Let the teacher countenance, nay, praise, the untidy page (provided the untidiness is due to careful thinking, not to careless writing), and he will find his pupils falling into a habit of self-criticism. If the writing has become illegible the piece should, of course, be re-written. The stages of a composition exercise are, therefore, three : preparation, rough draft, and final copy. And they may require three distinct lessons, or any two sequent stages may occupy one lesson, or any one stage may spread over many lessons." To put it briefly, the pupil must learn what Pope called the last and greatest art—the art to blot.

The next question is that of quantity : how

much time should be devoted to written composition? and how many words should be written during that time? It will be observed that the Harvard-Newton rules require 150 words in eighty minutes, and make no allowance for age: children of ten are expected to write as much in the given time as youths and maidens of sixteen. We, on the other hand, exact a higher rate of output, and we exact it on a sliding scale. Realizing that younger children think more slowly and write more slowly than older children, we demand more and more from our pupils as their years advance. The belief implied in the American scheme seems to be that though the pupil as he grows older will spend less time in actual writing, he will spend more time in making sure of his facts and in revising his script. We must not, however, assume that 150 words represents the average per week for American schools; it certainly does not represent the average for higher schools. According to a report issued in 1913 by the Modern Language Association of America, a report based on returns from ninety-three high schools and ninety-six colleges, the amount actually written averages for high schools 380 words a week throughout the year, and for colleges 630 words. The report suggests as ideal averages 430 and 680 words respectively. I know of no similar investigation in England, but these numbers seem to accord roughly with the practice in our own schools for higher education.

Whether it were wise to increase or to reduce the amount of written composition in our schools, is a question on which my own mind is open ; but there are other questions on which it is—for the present—shut. I hold it desirable, for instance, to abate the drudgery of marking ; and I hold it desirable to readjust the ratio of oral to written composition. That the conscientious teacher of English should consume the midnight oil in the marking of essays would not much matter, did he not at the same time unduly consume his own nervous force—and consume it unprofitably. For rarely does the essayist trouble himself about corrections and advice : he is generally content if he escapes open censure. At any rate the benefit is incommensurate with the labour. If the teacher takes twice the time over marking, the pupil does not get twice the benefit. Moreover, there are various means, such as the training of individual pupils as markers, by which the teacher may profitably shift upon other shoulders the burden of marking.

As for the proportion that oral composition bears to written, it will be observed that the school reverses the relationship found in life. The most literary among us talks much more than he writes : the least literary does not write at all. And yet in our schools the amount of oral composition, especially with the older scholars, is inordinately small compared with the amount of written. It is by no means unlikely that by increasing the oral work and reducing the written we shall benefit even the written. There is, at any rate, presumptive evidence to that effect. Mr. J. F. Hosic [1] describes an experiment made in twenty-two high schools by a committee of the Illinois Association of Teachers of English. The course for the second semester of the ninth grade in these schools (that is, the second half of the first year) was taught in two ways to parallel classes : one class had written exercises only, the other a combination of two-thirds oral and one-third written. The outcome was distinctly favourable to the use of oral composition. The sections taking the combined course made greater progress in written composition than the sections that had confined their practice to written composition. " They were better at the end of the semester in thought-vigour, freedom, and interest than the others ; they were no worse in spelling and punctuation, and better in handwriting—indeed, the writing sections showed marked degeneration in all

---

[1] *The Essentials of Composition and Grammar*, by J. F. Hosic, pp. 98–9. See also Professor Adams's account of this experiment on pp. 53–4 of *The New Teaching*.

matters of mechanics." All this points to the obvious fact—a fact of which the observant teacher needs no convincing—that practice, whether in essay-writing, or in penmanship, or in anything else—does not necessarily bring improvement: no progress takes place unless practice is supported by a desire to improve, an effort to improve, and a general attitude of vigilance and self-criticism. It also points to the fact that although speaking and writing are partly independent functions, we cannot improve one of them without also improving the other.

Of recent years much stress has been laid on topics that bring imagination into play. A pupil is frequently called upon to write "The Auto-biography of a Penny," to complete a story already begun, or to describe circumstances and events of which he can form but the wildest conjecture. He is put, in fact, to write fiction. And this exercise is supposed to give greater scope for originality, and to yield a finer type of training, than the mere recording of facts or the bare description of things seen and heard. Be that as it may, we must not forget how exacting is our demand. We ask our children to do what few adults can do even tolerably well. All normal children can be taught to write lucid, straightforward prose; but not all can be taught to write imaginatively and beautifully about a broomstick. Swift could do it; Johnson could do it; but not lesser men. Some children, no doubt, with a natural gift for lying (in an artistic sense), love to give the rein to their imagination; but these fictitious exercises should not be too persistently pressed on the matter-of-fact child (a genius perhaps in his way) whose forte lies in giving a plain and vivid account of real things.

We expect too much originality from tyros. We prefer to see them getting both ideas and words out of their heads. If we supply them with ideas, we want them to supply their own words, forgetting that words are not evolved from within, but are absorbed from without. A wholly original language would be a wholly unintelligible language. Originality of style can mean nothing but a selection from among variant forms of speech common to a social group. But these variant forms must be known first. Before we become original we must be conventional: we must conform to the modes of speech current in our environment. And these modes of speech cannot be learnt *in abstracto*: they can only be learnt in conjunction with the ideas they are meant to convey. A recognition of this fact lies at the root of the educational system of the Parents National Educational Union. Miss Charlotte Mason, its founder and guiding spirit, holds that culture comes best through books.

A good book is the best teacher ; for the language in which the meaning is couched has been so carefully chosen that it conveys the meaning more fitly and more unforgettably than the teacher possibly can. The teacher who talks literature is rare : books that present information in good literary form are plentiful. Hence matter and form—ideas and words—should be taught together through the medium of books. Not text-books, but books—real books that can be read without tedium and without tears. And as matter and form go together, so too should reading and reproduction go together. They are the taking-in and the giving-out, the impression and expression, which constitute the rhythm by which knowledge is assimilated. As soon as a child has read a passage or a page (the unit is increased as he grows older) he has to write it out from memory. If he is too young to write, he has to reproduce it orally. And reproduction in the *ipsissima verba* of the text is encouraged. Always the exact words if possible ; if not, the nearest approach. Such is the creed of the P.N.E.U., and such its practice.

Here we have a system which seems admirably adapted for the imparting of parrot-knowledge— a system common enough in the dame schools of old, but long since discarded along with the hornbook, the slate, and Magnall's Questions—

a system which leaves no room for originality : the pupil is fed with ideas already wedded to language, so there is no searching in the mind for the fitting phrase or the inevitable word. And yet those teachers who have tried the scheme speak of it with ardour and admiration. They say that it has kindled their own enthusiasm as well as the children's, and particularly that it has gone far towards solving the problem of essay-writing ; for the children trained on it, when asked to write upon a new topic, say sensible things in suitable words and show some sense of style. And from what I have seen of the results of this system, the claims made for it are to a certain extent justified. There is no doubt about it : it succeeds—and succeeds in spite of grave defects. It succeeds because it recognizes the supremely important fact that good writing rests on the imitation of good models ; and if the imitation is conscious and deliberate, it is far more effective than that unconscious imitation in which we are content to put our trust. Many a great writer has known this truth and has acted on it. Stevenson, as is well known, has proclaimed it boldly and insistently ; has himself sedulously pursued it as a method ; has indeed said that the way of imitation is the only way.

It must not be argued that because books are good the " bookier " a book is the better it is.

K

Indeed the more a book resembles good talk, or the more directly and vividly it presents its meaning, the more suitable it is for school purposes —and, many of us would add, for every other purpose as well. The general tendency of a writer as he gets older (and presumably wiser) is to write more simply : he uses plainer words, shorter phrases, and sentences of simpler structure. This tendency is specially noticeable in the writings of Johnson and Ruskin. When Ruskin issued, in 1883, a revised edition of the second volume of *Modern Painters*, which he had first published thirty-seven years before, he split up a number of the longer sentences, and commented caustically in footnotes on several others. Here are some of his notes : " This terrific two-page sentence ! " " The literary art and pedantry of [this paragraph] are now very grievous to me." " Too fast and far again ! by much ; the impetus of phrase running away with me. See the mischief of fine writing." " A long, affected and obscure sentence, written in imitation of Hooker. A short sentence from Proverbs is the sum of it : ' How can one be warm alone ? ' " He refers in the text to " The Anschauung of the Germans," and appends this note : " I have not the least idea now what the ' Anschauung ' of the Germans is ; and whatever it may be, beg my pupils to have nothing to do with it." It will be seen therefore that a wide acquaintance with books will not necessarily make us more bookish. Still, Russell Lowell's warning is not out of place: "That we should all be made to talk like books is the danger with which we are threatened by the Universal Schoolmaster, who does his best to enslave the minds and memories of his victims to what he esteems the best models of English composition, that is to say, to the writers whose style is faultily correct and has no blood-warmth in it. No language after it has faded into *diction*, none that cannot suck up the feeding juices secreted for it in the rich mother-earth of common folk, can bring forth a sound and lusty book. True vigour and heartiness of phrase do not pass from page to page, but from man to man."

The Englishman has a deep-rooted belief that the study of the ancient classics has a unique effect on one's literary style: it chastens and dignifies it as nothing else can. It was, according to Walter Bagehot, commonly thought in the eighteenth century that before a man can write good English he must first learn to write bad Latin. The opinion still survives—though no insistence is made on the badness of the Latin. We all fancy we can detect distinguishing points of merit in the writings of our friends who have received a classical training. We see in their sentences a certain fitness and seemliness—

a nice regard for the etymological meaning of words; a sense of rhythm, balance, and syntactical structure. We think of the aged Newman piously toiling at his daily task of Latin prose; we think of the golden age of English oratory where no speech in Parliament was complete without its Latin quotation; we think of the writers of the eighteenth century, who, whatever Bagehot may say, certainly wrote good English prose; and our faith in the classics is strengthened and our hearts comforted.

Then to disturb our peace of mind come the American educational psychologists with their irritating habit of challenging our most cherished beliefs, and they calmly put the matter to the test of experiment. The curious reader will find the result of this probing into vested opinion set forth in Chapter XIV of Starch's *Educational Psychology*. Three or four separate researches are described and explained with a full accompaniment of tables, graphs, and correlation coefficients. This is the conclusion reached by Mr. M. J. Wilcox, one of the researchers: "It seems evident, so far as the Iowa City and Cedar Rapids high schools are concerned, that the frequently demonstrated superiority of students who have had Latin is not due to the special discipline or training secured in the study of Latin. It is probably due to the fact that, as

a whole, the students who elect Latin are somewhat superior to those who refuse to take it."
Dr. Starch himself, investigating the effect on
written English of the study of foreign languages
as a whole (making no discrimination between
ancient and modern), sums up thus : " The conclusion seems, therefore, unavoidable that the
difference in ability in English composition is
due practically entirely to a difference in original
ability and only to a slight or no extent to the
training in foreign languages."

The only investigation that gives positive
evidence in favour of Latin was not concerned
with the teaching of Latin as such, but with
the teaching of Latin with special emphasis on
the derivation of English words from Latin
words. This is the old familiar Latin roots,
served not as a separate dish, but with a proper
dressing of grammar and text. Latin roots have
always been an object of scorn and derision to
classical scholars. D'Arcy Thompson says in his
Daydreams : " I heard, only a few days since,
that our girls were fed upon *Latin roots.* I
asked through what process of cookery these
roots might have passed. I was informed that
they were invariably given raw. Such indigestible food I knew to be fit only for pigs."
But then D'Arcy Thompson's interests were
centred in Latin and Greek literature, not English

prose; and his strictures on the study of derivations are clearly prejudiced.

Although it cannot be claimed that these few experiments settle the question, it must be admitted that they successfully unsettle it: we can no longer rest quite comfortably in the belief that if we look after our classical education all will be well; that if we labour at Latin prose composition a graceful English style will be our unfailing reward.

CHAPTER XIII

THE MAKING OF CRITICS

THE natural boy does not take kindly the complaints made about his English. They often seem to him the veriest hair-splitting; his language serves his own rough purpose well enough: what more is needed? Time and circumstance will gradually teach him what more is needed; he will observe that people (including himself) can rarely say exactly what they want to say: they fail to give the meaning, the whole meaning, and nothing but the meaning. He will further notice that people sometimes express themselves neatly and sometimes clumsily—that language may, in fact, become a fine art as well as a useful art. Time and circumstance will teach him this, but they need a little assistance; and the teacher would do well to press upon the pupil the need for careful and gracious speech; to cultivate in him a habit of criticism, and to rouse a sense of responsibility for maintaining the orderliness and prestige of our common heritage, the mother tongue. Unfortunately the old grammatical exercises are of little use for this purpose; partly because they are worked mechanically, and partly because the more serious and the more common defects of diction are not sins against grammar in the narrow sense, but sins against those broader laws of linguistic expression which school grammars leave out. A lad who has at last, not without a healthy resistance on his part, succumbed to the habit of parsing will cheerfully parse the most ungrammatical of sentences without any comment on its incorrectness. As for the broader laws of linguistic expression, these will be exemplified in the account which follows of the development of literary criticism in modern times.

The study of English grew under the shadow of the study of Latin. It was the Latin grammar that determined how it should grow and where it should stop. The first grammar written in English (Lily's, 1513) was a Latin grammar, and the *Grammar of the English Tongue* which Johnson put in the preface of his Dictionary was little more than a broken reflexion of a Latin grammar. He neither defined nor explained any of his terms, for he assumed that his readers were already acquainted with them. And when he came to deal with these terms in his Dictionary he borrowed his definitions (excellent definitions they are, by the way) from Clark's *Latin Grammar*.

It was left for two Scottish divines, Dr. George Campbell and Dr. Hugh Blair, to break away from the Latin grammar. Calling their subject Rhetoric they restored some of the jettisoned parts of the old grammars of Greece and Rome, and laid down certain canons of criticism and of literary taste which continue to be of some service unto this day. The Rhetoric of Campbell (1776) and of Blair (1783) was the whetstone on which the critics of the nineteenth century sharpened their swords; and it was the touchstone they used for the testing of the King's English. Dr. Hugh Blair, who seems to have been the more forceful personality of the two, was an outstanding figure in the intellectual life of Edinburgh in the eighteenth century. Boswell attended his lectures on Rhetoric and heard him mimic the style of Dr. Johnson. Johnson himself held him in high esteem. "I love Blair's sermons" (Blair was an inveterate sermon-writer), he says to Sir Joshua Reynolds. "I love Blair's sermons. Though the dog is a Scotchman, and a Presbyterian, and everything he should not be, I was the first to praise them." Posterity has not confirmed the Great Cham's judgment; for Blair's sermons are forgotten and his Lectures on Rhetoric have long been out of print. Still he said some good things, and said them well. The prophecy that the man who reached the North Pole would find a Scotchman sitting on it was not in point of fact fulfilled, but the Scot has an exasperating way of anticipating us elsewhere. What many of us have laboriously tried to say about language, Blair has already said quite neatly and compactly : " They who are learning to compose and arrange their sentences with accuracy and order, are learning, at the same time, to think with accuracy and order."

This quotation from Blair served as a motto for the title-page of a book whose author was destined to become as closely associated in the English mind with grammar as Edward Cocker with arithmetic. Lindley Murray differed in many ways from his predecessors : he was not an Englishman, nor a schoolmaster, nor an ecclesiastic. It was an accident that brought him to England—an accident of health—and it was an accident that made him a grammarian—an accident of friendship. He was an American lawyer who, having made a comfortable fortune by his calling, crossed the Atlantic in 1784 for the sake of his health. He was nearly forty when he left New York for old York (he settled down within a mile of the ancient city), and he lived for another forty years the life of a recluse. Indeed, for the last sixteen years he never left the house. A Quaker by religion, he was a man of a singularly sweet and gentle nature, who lived simply, and gave to charity all the profits of his literary work. It is doubtful whether he ever saw the inside of an English school, except perhaps that of a certain Quaker school for young ladies, with whose teachers he had formed a friendship. He spent most of his time in writing religious books—exhortations to piety and good works. Nobody read these books apparently; but everybody read, or pretended to have read, the grammar that he was induced to write by the mistresses at the little Quaker seminary in York. This grammar came out in 1795, and in various forms, abridged and extended, ran through a fabulous number of editions. It became *the* English grammar. As one reads it to-day, especially if one reads it in the final two-volume edition, it strikes one as being surprisingly modern. We have not improved much on Lindley Murray.

The most interesting part of Murray's book, and the most significant from our point of view, is the " Appendix : containing Rules and Observations for assisting Young Persons to write with Perspicuity and Accuracy; to be studied after they have acquired a competent Knowledge of English Grammar." He leads off with a quotation from Quintilian (" *Non solum ut intelligere possit, sed ne omnino possit non intelligere, curandum* "), and asserts boldly that " Perspicuity is the fundamental quality of style." Then he presents us with a series of rules gained from boiling down the works of Blair and Campbell and those of a few ancient authorities ; rules that, excellent as they are in the main, often reflect the weaknesses of the Scottish Rhetoricians. For the Scottish Rhetoricians took the narrow view of regarding Addison, Pope, and Swift as the sole models of English style.

Lindley Murray defines English grammar as " the art of speaking and writing the English language with propriety." *Propriety* is for him *le mot juste :* it strikes the key-note of his character and intellect. For in everything he is egregiously proper, with an occasional touch of the old maid. We detect in his writings, mingled with much sterner stuff, a faint odour of lavender and a slight suggestion of " prisms and prunes." He advises his readers to " avoid *low expressions :* such as topsy-turvy, hurly-burly, pellmell ; currying favour with a person ; dancing attendance on the great." He describes the phrase, " left to shift for themselves," as rather low, and too much in the familiar style to be proper in a grave treatise. The rules he lays down for securing euphony, a quality he much affects, would drive a modern writer to distraction. He thinks long words more agreeable to the ear than monosyllables, and finds some phonic reason or other for objecting to such words as, *tender-heartedness*, *chronicles*, *primarily*, and *farriery*. But Lindley Murray's rules need not trouble us much, for—as we shall presently see—he was unable to keep them himself. He realized the difficulty of the subject ; but the steps he took to mitigate the difficulty will astonish the modern student of child nature. To quote a passage from the advertisement to the third octavo edition : " He also ventures to presume, that the numerous exemplifications, of a moral and improving nature, with which all the editions of the work are interspersed ; and the short subsidiary disquisitions of the present edition ; will afford some relief to the subject of grammar, and render it less dry and uninteresting to the student. Perhaps they will be found to contribute, in some degree, to invite and encourage him to acquire an art, which in its own nature, does not, to young minds especially, present many attractions."

Lindley Murray has been called the father of English grammar. He did not fully deserve the title, for what he really did was to adopt a slovenly, foreign-looking child, tidy him up and make him look English. A quarter of a century later William Cobbett tried to give the child a new guise—and succeeded. Cobbett's Grammar stands by itself : there is no other like it. I have known unsophisticated adults take it up and read it from cover to cover. Written by a self-made man, it has taken part in the making of many another self-made man. Its title-page is full of promise : " A Grammar of the English Language, in a Series of Letters. Intended for the Use of Schools and of Young Persons in general ; but more especially for the Use of Soldiers, Sailors, Apprentices, and Plough-boys. By William Cobbett. To which are added, Six Lessons, intended to prevent Statesmen from using false grammar, and from writing in an awkward manner. London, 1818." The following is extracted from his own advertisement of the fifth edition (1823) : " He ventures to say that, from this book any person, however illiterate, will be enabled to write correctly in less time than is generally bestowed upon learning the first rudiments of spelling. . . . The author, when he first put forth this book, threw it down as a challenge to all the Reviewers, all the Colleges, and all the Universities. He was well aware whom he had to contend with. He was well aware of the infinite pains that would be taken to shut the door of *Schools* against his book ; but it is curious enough, that, while the school-masters themselves have, in most cases, been afraid to put it into the hands of their scholars, lest they should incur the displeasure of the rich and the powerful, those masters do not scruple to use it for the *teaching of themselves*, in which respect, they certainly act very wisely. The day will come, when this Grammar will be in use throughout the kingdom, to the exclusion of all others." There we have William Cobbett, a soldier once, a fighter always, confident of himself, mistrustful of others, ever " agin the Government," full of prickles and prejudices ; yet not altogether an unlovable man. He at any rate compels respect for the vigour of his thought and the aptness and forcefulness of his prose.

While Lindley Murray relieved the dulness of his pages with moral maxims, William Cobbett preferred the following method of enlivening his letters to his little son : " The nominative is frequently a noun of *multitude ;* as *mob, parliament, gang.*" " We may say : ' The gang of borough-tyrants *is* cruel ' ; or, that ' the gang of borough-tyrants *are* cruel ' ; but if we go on to speak of their notoriously brutal ignorance, we must not say : ' The gang of borough-tyrants *is* cruel, and *are* notoriously as ignorant as brutes.' We must use *is* in both places, or *are* in both places." " It is a very common parliament-house phrase, and, therefore, presumptively corrupt." " The frequent use of abbreviations is always a mark of slovenliness and of vulgarity. I have known Lords abbreviate almost the half of their words : it was, very likely, because they did not know how to spell them to the end."

The most characteristic part of Cobbett's Grammar appears towards the close, where he puts certain selected writings and speeches under a microscopic examination. Letter XXI deals with " Specimens of false Grammar, taken from the writings of Doctor Johnson and from those of Doctor Watts." Cobbett claims to have discovered about two hundred grammatical errors in Johnson's *Lives of the Poets ;* but he limits himself in his Grammar to criticism of *The Rambler* since Johnson himself had corrected it and revised it with extraordinary care, having made, so it is said, six thousand corrections before the work was printed in volumes. Here is a sample criticism. Johnson wrote in *The Rambler No.* 1 : " If I am not commended *for* the beauty of my works, I may be pardoned *for* their brevity." On this Cobbett remarks : " We may commend him *for* the beauty of his works ; and we may pardon him *for* their brevity, if we deem the brevity *a fault ;* but this is not what he means. He means that, at any rate, he shall have the *merit* of brevity : ' If I am not commended for the beauty of my works, I may hope to be pardoned *on account of* their brevity.' This was what the Doctor meant."

Letter XXII is entitled, "Errors and Nonsense in a King's Speech." The speech in question was read in Parliament on the 8th of November, 1814. There was not, according to Cobbett, a single sentence in the whole speech that was free from error. I give his comments on the second sentence, which reads thus : " It *would have given* me great satisfaction to *have been enabled* to *communicate* to you the *termination* of the war between this country and the United States of America." He points out that *to have been enabled* should be *to be enabled*, and that to *communicate* a *termination* is pure nonsense, since we can only communicate or share what we ourselves possess.

The last Letter contains the six lessons to statesmen. They consist of shrewd and caustic criticisms on important speeches made by members of Parliament. One speech begins : " I *continue* to receive from Foreign Powers the *strongest* assurances of their friendly disposition towards this country." Cobbett asks how the speaker can receive *the strongest* assurances more than once.

It seems to be the common fate of all grammarians to be taken to task sooner or later for their bad grammar. Lindley Murray was fortunate; for although Cobbett dealt him a few casual blows, his real castigation did not come till

L

long after he was dead. Cobbett himself was attacked at once in a booklet of sixty-four pages, published anonymously. The only shrewdness the writer showed was in withholding his name (Cobbett was too dangerous an opponent to meet openly); the criticisms themselves were so puerile that Cobbett took no notice of them.

A new departure was marked by the publication, in 1863, of *The Queen's English*, by Henry Alford, Dean of Canterbury. Previous critics had, as a rule, confined their censure to the lapses of the great—the failure of renowned writers and speakers to conform to certain rules laid down by grammarians. The speech of the common people, the private citizens who spoke the King's English naïvely, was either ignored or spoken of with contempt. Even Cobbett, with all his professions of regard for soldiers, sailors, and plough-boys, speaks disrespectfully of chambermaids, classing them as corrupters of English with " members of the House of Commons and learned Doctors." It was the grammarian whom the critics looked to for light and leading : he was their standard authority ; he was their final arbiter. But Dean Alford refused to accept this view : he changed, in fact, the court of appeal. Instead of appealing to the grammarians against the usage of writers and speakers, he appealed to common sense and popular usage against the grammarians. He refused to accept the ruling of Lindley Murray against the pen of Shakespeare and the voice of King Demos. To use his own words, " Most of the grammars, and rules, and applications of rules, now so commonly made for our language, are in reality not contributions towards its purity, but main instruments of its deterioration." He notes that there are among grammarians honourable exceptions.

Whenever the idiom of the people does not violate common sense he puts forth a plea on its behalf. He defends the phrase, " It is me," for instance, on the ground that *me* is here a secondary nominative, like *moi* in French. He argues that "the three first Gospels " is better English than " the first three Gospels." He is very severe (and rightly so, I think) on those who depreciate the language and grammar of the Authorized Version of the Scriptures. " I would recommend them," he says, " to try the experiment of amending that language. They may then find that what the translators themselves once said is true. A story is told, that they had a recommendation from a correspondent to alter a certain word in their version, giving *five* sufficient reasons for the change. They are said to have replied that they had already considered the matter, and had *fifteen* sufficient reasons *against* the change."

The reader will, no doubt, sympathize with the Dean when he girds at the pedantic rules laid down for the position of *only* in the sentence. The natural tendency seems to be to place *only* before the verb, even though it appears *on analysis* to limit the object of the verb. If, for instance, I say, "I only had an apple for lunch to-day," the grammarian will take me to task for saying what I don't mean. He argues that *only* modifies *had*, and that I exclude by my statement all possibilities except *having* the apple; that I imply that I did not cook it, or peel it, or bite it, or do anything with it except possess it. The correct form is, "I had only an apple (or, an apple only) for lunch to-day," for *only* limits *apple*, and the possibility I intend to exclude is, "I had an apple plus something else for lunch to-day." This is the grammarian's account of the matter, and Dean Alford admits that, strictly speaking, he is right, and the Dean in consequence takes refuge in the position that the more exact English is not necessarily the better English. Now Dean Alford ought not to have made that admission : I contend that the grammarian is wrong. He is wrong because he makes the fatal and fundamental mistake of thinking that the meaning of a sentence when it is spoken or heard is no less and no more than the sum total of the meanings into which it can be analyzed. It is the mistake of thinking the dissected flower is the same thing as the undissected flower ; of thinking that we can cut it to pieces without destroying its life, and can put the pieces together again and restore the original flower. As a matter of fact, a simple sentence is the expression of a single pulse of thought, the movement of which appears in the predicate. The predicate, the logical and undivided predicate, represents thought upon the wing, and has a peculiar dynamic unity of its own. In the sentence under discussion, "had-an-apple-for-lunch-to-day" must be taken as a whole, and it is this whole that is modified by *only*. The assertion that the sentence really denies and excludes is, " I had a more substantial lunch than an apple to-day." Be that as it may, the original sentence, " I only had an apple for lunch to-day," the sentence as it naturally falls from the lips of the plain man, has no ambiguity whatever about it : it cannot be misunderstood except by a mind debauched by an excess of grammar.

Dean Alford broke new ground in another direction. He was the first to make a serious attack on journalese, the first to point out that attempts at fine writing on the part of the half-educated often lead to the gross misuse of words and the general corruption of the mother tongue. He was apparently the first to protest against the flagrant abuse of the word *individual*. "To use *individual* wrongly in the twentieth century," say the authors of *The King's English*, "stamps a writer, more definitely than almost any other single solecism, not as being generally ignorant and foolish, but as being without the literary sense." Quite so! in the twentieth century. But in the nineteenth century everybody used it wrongly, from Thomas Carlyle to Marie Corelli. And to detect something unnatural and wrong about red noses in a land where all noses were red, would be a mark of astuteness; to proclaim the discovery, a mark of courage. I believe the use of *individual* for *person* pure and simple, with no suggestion of contrast with a group or combination of persons, arose from the Victorian straining after what Mr. Fowler calls "polysyllabic humour." *Individual* had a comic implication. When a Victorian wanted to be funny he called a nose an olfactory organ, and its possessor an individual. There seems to be a tendency of late years to use the word in scientific writings in a sense that is incorrect, without the excuse of being funny.

Other journalistic words and phrases objected to by the Dean are *female* for *woman*, *party* for *man, the rising generation* for *children, proceed* for *go, partake* for *eat* (even when the whole is eaten), *evince* for *show, commence* for *begin, avocation* for *calling, locality* for *place,* and so forth. He asserts that " most of the people of the place," would be regarded as a terrible vulgarism, and would be altered into " the majority of the residents in the locality."

As soon as Dean Alford's book appeared (or rather the articles in *Good Words* which he afterwards put together to form his book), he was admonished by Mr. George Washington Moon for breaking his own rules and for writing atrociously bad English himself. *The Queen's English* by Alford was followed by *The Dean's English* by Moon. And the Dean's English was held up to ridicule and scorn. Moon had a remarkably sharp ear for verbal infelicities, and a remarkably keen eye for the infraction of any rule of grammar that anybody had ever formulated. Several times did he catch the Dean tripping. The Dean wrote : " If with your inferiors, speak no coarser than usual ; if with your superiors, no finer," and Moon rebuked him for using adjectives for adverbs. The Dean wrote : " A man does not lose his mother now in the papers " ; and Moon wondered how she could get lost there. The Dean wrote : " Sometimes the editors of our papers fall, from their ignorance, into absurd mistakes "; and Moon pointed out that people could not fall from ignorance, but could only rise from it. These examples will give the reader an idea of the quality of Moon's criticisms.

Moon made merry with one of the Dean's paragraphs, which contained so many nouns and pronouns that it was possible to give it a large number of different meanings. Moon, in fact, discovered 10,240. Happily, he did not give all these meanings: he merely worked out the number by counting the combinations. To substitute a simpler instance, Moon argues that such a sentence as, "When John meets his uncle he always lifts his hat," is ambiguous; for it admits of four interpretations. We are not told whether John lifts John's hat, or John lifts his uncle's hat, or the uncle lifts the uncle's hat, or the uncle lifts John's hat. The Dean's reply to this criticism was that he did not write for idiots. This made Moon very angry; and when the Dean explained that the remark was not intended for him personally, but for a hypothetical person, Moon returned vigorously to the attack, asserting that his blows were not aimed at Dean Alford personally, but at a hypothetical dean.

In his first reply the Dean started a sentence with the words, "The one rule of all others which he cites . . ." and Moon was not slow to take advantage of the opening. He inquired how a rule could be of, or among, other rules; and here he made a hit, a palpable hit. And thus the petty quarrel dragged on. Many thought that Moon won. What he really did was to win on the small points and lose on the large issues. *The Queen's English* stands as an eminently readable book, written in idiomatic English, full of sound common sense, and showing evidence of a genuine love of the vulgar tongue which the Prayer-Book adjures us to teach our children. Moon, on the other hand, right as he often was in detail, took up a position which was fundamentally wrong. He would cavil on the ninth part of a hair and solemnly quote the Scottish rhetoricians in support of his cavilling. While Alford took the biological view of language, regarding it as a living, growing, changing thing, Moon took the mechanical or mathematical view: making no distinction between the living sentence and the dead words, he measured everything up by rule and compass.

The Dean's English sold so well that Moon was encouraged to try again; and he soon brought out another book, which he called *Bad English*. His chief victim this time was Lindley Murray. This did not matter very much, for Lindley Murray, in a sense, deserved his trouncing; moreover, he was dead and did not mind it. Moon undertook to show that " in the very volume in which he [Lindley Murray] laid down his rules, he frequently expressed himself ungrammatically." He further maintained that " almost every kind of fault in composition may be found in Lindley Murray's own writings." I will give two of Moon's instances, which my reader is invited to try his hand at correcting. (1) " Many sentences are miserably mangled, and the force of the emphasis totally lost." (2) " The importance of obtaining, in early life, a clear, distinct, and accurate knowledge. . . ." The error in the first the reader has, no doubt, already guessed : the *are* which is understood between *emphasis* and *totally* should be *is*. But has the reader found the error in the second ? I myself failed completely. Here is the solution. Supplying each ellipsis, we get " *a* clear, [*a*] distinct, and [*a*] accurate knowledge." Wonderful ! is it not ? But Lindley Murray has himself to blame. He says, " When a different form of the article is requisite, the article is also properly repeated : as, ' *A* house and *an* orchard ' ; instead of ' A house and orchard.' "

Only could not fail to arouse comment. This easy and natural sentence of Lindley Murray's, " When the voice is only suspended for a moment . . ." should, according to Moon, have been, " When the voice is suspended for only a moment. . . ." Several similar instances are cited. Moon's conclusion is that Lindley Murray wrote worse than his rules; the just conclusion is that he wrote better than his rules.

Moon wrote many other books besides these, one of them containing an epic poem called *Elijah the Prophet*; but he will always be remembered as the man who wrote *The Dean's English*. Quite appropriately, he shines by reflected glory.

The crusade started in England by Dean Alford was taken up in America by James Russell Lowell. Lowell saw an enemy in the pedagogue on one side, and in the journalist on the other. He says in the *Biglow Papers*, " While the schoolmaster has been busy starching our language and smoothing it flat with the mangle of a supposed classical authority, the newspaper reporter has been doing even more harm by stretching and swelling it to suit his occasions." He proceeds to give a list of some of the changes he has noticed in newspaper style. Here is one. Where the old writer would say, " A bystander advised," the modern writer says, " One of those omnipresent characters who, as if in pursuance of some previous arrangement, are certain to be encountered in the vicinity when an accident occurs, ventured the suggestion."

As a result of these strictures, and of sporadic criticisms in the Press, there grew up in England towards the close of the nineteenth century a general feeling that certain words and phrases offended against either grammar or good taste. There were degrees in the offending. To use *averse to* was a venial offence; but to use *and which* wrongly was beyond forgiveness. Few knew why. A civil servant who was once reprimanded by his chief for writing *and which* in a memorandum defended himself by saying that he had there used it as an extension of the predicate—an explanation that was at once accepted. It was also at that time held (on insufficient grounds) that the guilt of corrupting the language rested mainly on the heads of a few journals and a few writers. This limerick of the period points to the chief scapegoats :

> "A vicar there was of Endellion,
>   Who drove all his flock to rebellion;
>   His style if you please
>   Was Telegraphese,
> And his grammar was Marie Corellian."

In the year 1904 was published *The King's English*, the standard book on the negative virtues of English prose—on the common faults of grammar and style to be found in modern books and modern newspapers. That *The King's English*, by Messrs. H. W. and F. G. Fowler, is a masterpiece in a small way, is as certain as that Johnson's Dictionary is a masterpiece in a large way. For

many a long year it will be the *vade mecum* of
the critic, and the book of reference to which
the writer will turn in trepidation whenever his
English is called into question. As, however,
one reads it through (it is eminently readable—
more readable than rememberable), and finds
the number of great writers who constantly
stumble, one cannot but ask : Who, then, can
be saved ? Laudable as is the attempt to bring
more law and order into English prose—to preserve its purity and enhance its efficiency—the
general effect of the book on the amateur is to
depress. He feels that if the path of the man
who aspires to write is so beset with pitfalls,
he were wise not to fare forth at all. In learning about the pitfalls he will have exhausted
his resources of time and enthusiasm. He will
resemble the man in one of Stephen Leacock's
books who had acquired the health habit. As
soon as he got home in the evening he began
exercising his muscles to clear his brain. When
his brain was quite clear it was time to go to
bed.

Looked at in another way, however, *The King's
English* is a reassuring and stimulating book. If
Scott and Lamb and Dickens and George Eliot
fall so far short of perfection in the technique
of letters—of perfection as the grammarian con-
ceives it—it is clear that their greatness rests on

certain positive qualities of style and subject-matter, qualities which the authors of *The King's English* frankly admit they have not touched. Let the reader, therefore, take heart of grace. If he has something vital to say, something that is worth saying, let him, in Heaven's name, say it with all the sincerity he can compass, never doubting that his message will reach home, even though his grammar be a little faulty and his style a little lax. Style (in the narrower sense) will not save the man who has nothing to say; nor will its absence mar him if he has something of himself to impart. If, indeed, he succeeds in imparting something of himself he will already have achieved style in that larger and deeper sense which Buffon had in mind when he said that style was the man.

Sir Arthur Quiller-Couch, in his Oxford Lectures on *The Art of Writing*, published in 1916, lays great stress on practice. "Literature," he says, "is not a mere science, to be studied; but an art, to be practised." And practice should aim at securing four cardinal qualities: appropriateness, perspicuity, accuracy, and persuasiveness. So far there is nothing new (Lindley Murray said the same thing over a hundred years ago), but the way in which Sir Arthur deals with the matter is both new and charming. His chapter on Jargon is a delight. Jargon is not journalese. Though the two overlap and "have a knack of assimilating each other's vices," jargon has a special province of its own. The journalist is, in his way, an artist. He daubs, it is true; but he daubs with a professional zeal; "he is trying all the while to embellish our poor language, to make it more floriferous, more poetical." "No such gusto marks the practitioners of Jargon"; their instinct is "to save everything, especially trouble." The journalist strains after effect, the jargonist shelters himself in the conventional. Jargon is, according to Sir Arthur, becoming the language of Parliament, County Councils, Syndicates, Committees, and Commercial Firms. When a Minister of the Crown says in the House of Commons, "The answer to the question is in the negative," he is talking jargon. When the Clerk of a Board of Guardians minutes that: "In the case of John Jenkins, deceased, the coffin provided was of the usual character," he is writing jargon.

The two main vices of jargon are the use of "circumlocution rather than short, straight speech," and the habitual choice of vague, woolly, abstract nouns instead of concrete ones. To avoid these vices the author gives a few rough rules. "The first is: Whenever in your reading you come across one of these words, *case, instance, character, nature, condition, persuasion, degree—*

whenever in writing your pen betrays you to one or another of them—pull yourself up and take thought." For another rule : " Train your suspicions to bristle up whenever you come upon ' as regards,' ' with regard to,' ' in respect of,' ' in connection with,' ' according as to whether,' and the like. They are all dodges of jargon, circumlocutions for evading this or that simple statement. . . . You should never use them."

In the same vein is written an essay on " The Decay of Syntax," by Mr. R. W. Chapman (1918). Mr. Chapman thinks that ever since the eighteenth century, which was the golden age, English prose has been falling to pieces. The only modern writers (he names five) who construct good prose " have clearly formed their style by the study of seventeenth and eighteenth-century models ; and as prose style must be formed upon models, their prose is good because their models are good." In other words, he harks back to the ideals of Campbell and Blair. He contends that " the modern sentence has neither rhythm nor structure ; it goes on till it drops." The two words *case* and *instance* move him to scorn, as they do Sir Arthur Quiller-Couch. He says, " The man who writes ' instances of premature mortality are more frequent in the case of men than in the case of women,' when he means that more men die young than women, sins against the light."

The jargon against which these critics rail is, as a rule, written in reports, minutes, memoranda, and business letters. It is the special malady of official English. Official English often departs from ordinary English in unexpected ways, and persists in its own path in spite of protest. The word *as*, for instance, has acquired a wide vogue in official circles. Wherever *as* can be put in, in it goes. And often it gets into places where it has no business to be. A man in the public service used to draw his salary *from* a certain date; now he draws it *as from* a certain date. Time was when officials would refer to " the relationship between one department and another "; now they call it " the relationship *as* between one department and another." Agenda papers often include as an item : " To consider as to the question of . . ." If this sort of interpolation between the verb and its object were extended to ordinary speech, a man would no longer " eat his dinner," but " eat as to his dinner "; or, to make the parallel complete, " eat as to the diet of his dinner."

Considering the general predilection for *as*, it is curious to note the tendency of officials to reject *as soon as* in favour of *immediately*, used as a conjunction. Instead of, " As soon as you receive this letter . . ." they write, " Immediately you receive this letter . . ."

M

A peculiar change has recently taken place in the manner of naming the date on which a year ends. It used to take the form, "The year ending June 30th," whether the 30th of June were past or to come. Nowadays if the date be past the phrase used is, "The year ended June 30th." This is a solecism. It gains its plausibility from the fact that the verb "to end" is both active and neuter—it is used both transitively and intransitively. In reference to periods of time, such as a year or a month, it is clearly used intransitively. The year ends in its own time : it is not ended by somebody's fiat. It is not snuffed out : it simply runs out. In grammatical form "the year ends" is identical with "the boy speaks"; and as "the boy speaking yesterday" is right, and "the boy spoken yesterday" wrong, so is "the year ending yesterday" right, and "the year ended yesterday" wrong—wrong, that is, when *ended* is a participle.

But a truce to this one-sided pleading! Has the jargonist (if I may be pardoned the word) nothing to say for himself? The truth is, if the use of stereotyped phrases and vague, empty words makes a man a jargonist, then are we all jargonists. The man who says "Good morning!" or "How d'ye do?" to every acquaintance he meets in the street, is no less guilty of jargon than the merchant who dictates a few dozen letters straight off, each beginning: "Dear Sir, Your favour of *n*th inst. to hand." Each uses a formula, and uses it as a social convenience. Coleridge in his *Table Talk* tells a story of a verbal encounter he had with a Jew whom he heard shouting "Ogh Clo" in the street. "Pray," said Coleridge to him, "why can't you say 'old clothes' in a plain way, as I do now?" The Jew stopped, and looking very gravely at him, said in a clear and even fine accent, "Sir, I can say 'old clothes' as well as you can; but if you had to say so ten times a minute, for an hour together, you would say *Ogh Clo*, as I do now."

Here we have the secret of jargon: it saves energy. If the merchant mentioned above were to begin each letter with different words and in a different tone—an epigram in one, a quaint conceit in another, a grave admonition in a third —if he carefully weighed the wording of each sentence and each phrase, he would never get through his correspondence. If he puts brains into his English he will have to leave them out of his business. His opening formula ("Your favour of *n*th inst. to hand," or whatever else it may be) is a labour-saving device just as truly as a vacuum-cleaner is a labour-saving device; and why should such devices be commended in the realm of things and condemned in the realm of words? The formula indeed serves the merchant's purpose better than a phrase that will distract the recipient's attention from the real purport of the letter. The recipient accepts the formula as a sign of business courtesy, just as we accept a formal greeting in the street as a sign of social courtesy.

Let us consider another labour-saving phrase, a phrase in constant use among officials who have to deal with school accommodation. Instead of saying that a school is crowded, or that the demand for school places is greater than the supply, or that there are many names on the waiting list, they say that there is " pressure on the accommodation." This seems at first blush the veriest fustian. Yet any one who is concerned with getting children into school soon finds the convenience of the phrase. It admits of degrees (we can indicate the amount of pressure); it can apply to a district as well as to a school; and it can cover a variety of cases in which the differences are irrelevant to the issue. It is, in fact, a skeleton key which fits many locks.

Jargonists are of two types, the conscious and the unconscious—those who know they are using jargon and limit it to its proper sphere, and those who do not know they are using jargon and think they are using the King's English. It is only the unconscious jargonists who are dangerous; but as they are the stupider class, their influence is the lesser. The conscious jargonist is perfectly harmless; whether he be Charles Lamb, who wrote jargon in the India Office and wrote literature at home; or Kenneth Grahame, who was a jargonist at the Bank of England, and outside its precincts a writer of delicate and delightful prose. Mr. Augustine Birrell has often said, "The answer to this question is in the negative"; but this bowing of the knee to jargon does not prevent him from Birrelling even in the House of Commons.

We begin to suspect that the jargonist is not such an ass as he seems.

When we consider the jargonist's use of periphrastic prepositions, he comes out in a still more amiable light. While he uses formulas to save himself trouble, he uses long-tailed prepositions to save other people trouble. *As regards, with regard to, in respect of, in connection with*, the phrases that Sir Arthur Quiller-Couch would have us abjure, are primarily useful in making it easy for the ideas that follow them to enter the reader's mind. I will instance the use of that compound preposition of which there is at present an epidemic—*in connection with*. A circular which goes the rounds of Government offices will begin thus : " In connection with the supply of coal for the district . . ." *In connection with* serves the same purpose as those curious bladders which the Laputians used for smiting their fellow-citizens in order to attract their attention. Nay, more ; it is a string that pulls up into the mind the relevant topic. Or, to change the metaphor once more, it is a pathway that leads into what the logicians call " the universe of discourse." The reader thus gets at once into the heart of things. It is true that the circular is headed " Coal Supply," a title which seems to hint at what is coming, but the writer of the circular is actuated by the kindly motive of helping those who forget to read the heading. Perhaps the writer somewhat overdoes the business of helping the reader ; for the next paragraph leads off with : " In this connection . . ." He might perhaps have credited the reader with enough penetration to guess that if he were going to talk about something else—something entirely disconnected with the supply of coal, he would say it elsewhere. But he means well. What he virtually says is : " Now keep your mind fixed on the same subject ; I'm not going to wander off." His opinion of the reader's intelligence may not be high, but his intentions are kindly.

As for the vagueness of the phrase *in connection with* (or, to use the term now fashionable at

Oxford and Cambridge, its woolliness), it is in that very quality that its special virtue lies. We need vague (or woolly) terms to express vague (or woolly) relationships; and it is better to let a few prepositions specialize in vagueness rather than let quite definite prepositions serve vague purposes. Commercial travellers are wont to offend in this way. When a commercial traveller wishes to define his job, he says he "travels *in* soap," or in some other commodity. He, of course, means that he travels for the purpose of pushing the sale of a particular kind of soap; but not being a pedant, he says quite simply, "I travel in soap." And everybody knows what he means. But it was a pity to spoil *in* by making it woolly, when *in connection with* was already woolly.

And when we come to look closely into the matter, we find that there is something to be said for the modern use of *case*—the word so often pilloried by the critics of to-day. This word, too, is a picker-out of the essential theme: it isolates it and turns the limelight on it. Suppose I am discussing the fine arts, and point to a certain feature that is common to a number of them, such as the imitative function; and I then want to show that in music we have a notable exception; I do it by saying, "But in the case of music (no, Sir Arthur, I do *not* mean 'in the music-case ')—in the case of music there is nothing to imitate." Music is at once in the limelight. I admit that *the case of* may be omitted without serious loss ; but it cannot be omitted without some loss. To the modern mind the full phrase isolates and enforces better than the mere device of position.

The word *instance*, like the word *case*, can be used rightly as well as wrongly. Sir Arthur Quiller-Couch, who looks askance at it, uses it himself on page 68 of his book. It is only wrong when nothing is instanced and it is not known for certain to what it refers. As for the instance of the misuse of *instance* given by Mr. Chapman, I do not think it proves his point. Taking this sentence from Cobbett, " In numerous instances the farmers have ceased to farm for themselves," he says it is not clear whether Cobbett meant " many districts " or " many farmers." It *is* clear. Cobbett meant " many farmers."

There are varieties of jargon that can be defended on the score that they serve to maintain the dignity of an honourable calling. A younger son of a late Prime Minister entered the Civil Service. One day he was called to account for writing at the close of an official memorandum : " Please let me have an answer back quick." He was told that the proper phrase was : " Please expedite a reply." Whether you regard this piece of jargon as dignified or pompous will depend on whether you send it or receive it. At any rate, it keeps vulgarity at bay. On whatever side it errs it does not err on the side of slang and a slap-him-on-the-back familiarity. And unless some sort of barrier is raised against flippancy and frivolity, what is there to prevent a young blood from the University writing to a colleague old enough to be his father: " Buck up, old bean " ?

In the recent attacks on jargon it is implied that jargon is of modern growth and that it is still expanding. The truth is, there always has been jargon and there always will be. And it would be just as easy to find instances (or cases) of jargon on the decrease as of jargon on the increase. At any rate, there is often a tendency to narrow the field within which it is practised. Just as the powder and periwigs, the cocked hats and frogged coats, which were the common attire of the eighteenth century, became the garb of ceremonial and flunkeyism in the nineteenth and twentieth centuries, so have the empty formulas of the many become, in the course of time, the emptier formulas of the few. In the eighteenth century, the age towards which the reformers turn their faces, it was the custom for everybody to close his letters with the words, " Your most humble and obedient servant." Nowadays this epistolary style is confined to the highest officials in the Civil Service. The more manifestly high-handed and autocratic the functionary, the more punctilious is he in assuring us that he is our humble and obedient servant.

Having said what I can in defence of the jargonist, I must now leave him to his fate, with the advice that he should plead guilty to the rest of the charges that have been brought against him. There are perhaps extenuating circumstances, but not exonerating circumstances.

Those who complain about the decay of syntax, rather than the decay of accuracy in word and meaning—who say that the modern sentence has lost its rhythm and lost its structure—ascribe the cause to the modern habit of reading by the eye instead of reading by the ear. The trend of to-day is to use the eye more and the ear less. The cinema is replacing the theatre, and the laboratory the classroom. Even in the classroom itself the oral lesson in which the teacher talks and explains is gradually disappearing in favour of schemes of private study and individual pursuits. In the great world everybody reads, and reads silently. To nothing like the same extent as of yore do people go to church to hear sermons or to public places to hear speeches. When they go to theatres they prefer spectacular plays. The audience can no longer be properly called an audience : it has become a mere crowd of spectators. The outcome of all this is that a feeling for the beauty of speech as a series of articulate sounds is passing away, and with it goes a love for the melody and rhythm of good prose. The printed page has captured the eye and banished the ear ; it has ceased to be a suggester of the living voice : it has become a substitute for the living voice.

While the general trend of things is driving us towards a greater reliance on the eye and a lesser reliance on the ear, the American psychologists are conspiring to accelerate the trend : they are pushing on behind, so to speak. If we listen to them we shall cease reading in the good, solid, conscientious way of carefully plodding through a paragraph word by word, trying to squeeze the last ounce of meaning out of it. We must acquire the art of " skimming," as Professor Adams calls it. We must speed up the pace and, taking in the meaning purely through the eye, read as fast as we possibly can. To do this we must get rid of all intermediaries between the eye and the meaning. We must break ourselves of two bad habits—the habit of silently articulating the words as we read them, and the habit of imagining we hear them spoken. For these habits curb the onward rush of the mind, and make our reading and our understanding far slower than they need be. The very habit which the stylists deplore—the habit of reading through the eye—is the one which the Americans urge us to acquire in the interests of a get-wise-quick policy. They bring figures to prove that if we tear along through the page, although we shall spill a little of the meaning by the way, we shall arrive at the end with a larger quantity of meaning than the slow reader will have picked up in the same time—not in the same journey, but in the same time. Taking time into account, the skimmer always wins.

Whom are we to listen to, the psychologist (American) or the stylist? If the purpose of reading be to garner in ideas at the highest speed, irrespective of their quality, then the psychologist is right. But we cannot ignore the quality of the ideas gathered in; still less can we ignore the quality of the ideas left behind. For the ideas left behind are the ones that are most worth troubling about. They are the ideas that the reader is unfamiliar with, is unprepared for, is insensitive to; they are the only ideas which, if taken in, would make an appreciable change in his mental equipment. But as they fall upon the blind spots of his mind, he not only misses them: he is unaware that he has missed them. Moreover, the little things escape him. The little joke that the writer has tucked away in a corner, the subtle meaning he has tried to infuse into a phrase, the *nuances* and delicacies—all these are lost upon the skimmer. The inveterate skimmer, that is. Everybody skims occasionally. It is the only thing to do with journalism, whether it appears in newspapers or in books; but literature, whether it appears in newspapers or in books, is to be read; and read slowly. To skim the Essays of Charles Lamb is as unwise as to skim Euclid's *Elements of Geometry*.

This brings me to the second weakness in the psychologist's position. He assumes that the sole purpose of reading is the getting of knowledge. He leaves out the æsthetic purpose. He makes no distinction between the facts in the Newgate Calendar and the facts in the play of Hamlet; nor between the gospel according to Jeremy Bentham and the Gospel according to St. John. Good prose has a definite form—a form due to a deliberate choosing and placing of words—a form that manifests itself mainly in rhythm and melody; and rhythm and melody appeal not to the eye, but to the ear. If, therefore, a man reads a fine piece of prose purely through the eye, he will miss the very qualities that make it a fine piece of prose. And if he reads poetry through the eye, he will gain a few facts and lose all the poetry.

As for the pace at which a reader can assimilate

a piece of writing, whether poetry or prose, that depends partly on himself and partly on what he reads. Some writings should be sipped, some gulped, and some poured down the sink.

But we must not be unjust to the psychologist. He has rendered good service in challenging the efficiency of our reading habits and forcing us to examine them closely. He says that they are bad habits, that they are fixed at the outset by our methods of teaching reading, and that it is possible to mend them. But he must show us a better way of mending them than by destroying our sense of style. He probably will, if we give him enough time.

Grammarians find no difficulty in telling us what style is, but practitioners in the art of Letters are not so clear on the matter. Samuel Butler repudiates style altogether. He says in his *Note-Books:* " I should like to put it on record that I never took the smallest pains with my style, have never thought about it, and do not know or want to know whether it is a style at all or whether it is not, as I believe and hope, just common, simple straightforwardness. I cannot conceive how any man can take thought for his style without loss to himself and his readers." And yet he says in the previous paragraph : " A man may, and ought to take a great deal of pains to write clearly, tersely and euphemistically : he will write many sentences three or four times over—to do much more than this is worse than not re-writing at all: he will be at great pains to see that he does not repeat himself, to arrange his matter in the way that shall best enable the reader to master it, to cut out superfluous words and, even more, to eschew irrelevant matter: but in each case he will be thinking not of his own style, but of his reader's convenience." If this is not taking pains with one's style, I should like to know what is. The next sentence gives the key to the mystery: " Men like Newman and R. L. Stevenson seem to have taken pains to acquire what they call a style as a preliminary measure—as something that they had to form before their writings could be of any value." It was style as a preparatory gymnastic that Butler repudiated, not style as a principle of order, clearness and force.

Opinions differ as to the number of emendations a man should make in his writings. Cobbett would have us make none. He says to his son, " Never think of mending what you write. Let it go. No patching; no after-pointing. As your pen moves, bear constantly in mind, that it is making strokes which are to remain for ever." And again, " Use the first words that occur to you, and never attempt to alter a thought; for that which has come of itself into your mind is likely to pass into that of another more readily and with more effect than anything which you can, by reflection, invent." On the other hand, it is recorded that in a rough draft of one of Plato's Dialogues, found after his death, the first paragraph was written in seventy different forms. Between these two extremes authors range in every variety. Ruskin says in *Fiction Fair and Foul*, " A sentence of *Modern Painters* was often written four or five times over in my own hand, and tried in every word for perhaps an hour—perhaps a forenoon—before it was passed for the printer." These differences in opinion and differences in practice are not so great as at first sight they seem. All the writers quoted take pains to arrange their thoughts and words well; but some take the pains before putting pen to paper, and some after. Cobbett, for instance, assumes that a writer will ponder well what he has to say before attempting to say it. " Sit down," he says, " to write what you have thought, and not to think what you shall write."

To a few writers of the second half of the nineteenth century—to Pater, Newman, and Stevenson—style meant something much more intricate and complex than the style that was consciously practised by the writers of the eighteenth century. While it was the architecture of the sentence that mainly interested the eighteenth-century writers, it was the music of the sentence that mainly interested the nineteenth-century writers. Even in an age when few cared for music, the great writers of the eighteenth century were conspicuously unmusical. They did not, of course, ignore the articulatory and phonic aspects of the sentence, but they were mainly concerned with the avoidance of asperities. They were content with smoothness, with the absence of stuttering syllables and cacophonous phrases. They did not strive after (if indeed they were aware of) those positive merits of musical pattern that Stevenson so well describes in his essay on *Some Technical Elements of Style in Literature*. Still less did they consciously try to weave that quadruple web which gave Stevenson's own style its peculiar complexity.

It is at least a tenable theory that too much preoccupation with style robs one's writings of freshness and incisiveness ; that singleness of purpose is in the last resort better than straining after many qualities at once. Professor Miall, speaking as a scientist, praises plainness of speech. In his book, *Thirty Years of Teaching*, he commends those authors who wrote as they talked, and condemns " the allusive, conventionally elegant Latinism of Robertson and Gibbon, which has left a smear on much of the writing of the last and present century." " That style," he goes

N

on to say, " is now the mark of the least educated and worst bred—may it never come into favour again ! "

I have now brought under review the main attitudes towards style that have been adopted by modern critics and modern writers. It will, no doubt, be felt that many of the criticisms I have quoted are at least captious, if not sophistical ; that Johnson's sentence is better as it stands than Cobbett's emendation ; that Cobbett's sentence is no worse than the alteration that Mr. Chapman suggests ; that Lindley Murray's faults are better than Moon's corrections of those faults ; and that Dean Alford's English is on the whole quite as good as Moon's. It will be felt that the canons of criticism that guide the activities of one age shackle the activities of the next ; that if Rudyard Kipling were judged by the standards of Campbell and Blair he would be left outside the pale of literature. But in spite of all this— in spite of differences of opinion among writers of the same period, and in spite of changes that time has wrought in the standards of judgment, there are certain principles which are as valid to-day as they were when man first achieved articulate speech. Perspicuity is an indispensable factor in good speaking, said Quintilian nineteen hundred years ago ; perspicuity is the fundamental quality of style, said Lindley Murray a

century and a quarter ago; perspicuity is one
of the four essentials of good writing, says the
Professor of English Literature at the University
of Cambridge to-day.

This is only a sample. There are enough sound
principles to constitute a body of knowledge that
asks for recognition and a name. Scottish and
American scholars called it Rhetoric more than
a century ago; and Rhetoric it is called in those
countries to this day. It is the philosophy of
speaking and writing; it is the science of composition as distinct from the art of composition.
And it is this science that should, in my opinion,
take the place of grammar as part of the English
course in all our higher schools—the continuation
school, the secondary school, the training college,
and the University. It includes grammar, in the
narrow sense, but it broadens its boundaries. It
runs into logic in one direction and into philo-
logy in the other. It has many ramifications,
any one of which may be followed and become
the work of a lifetime. But in the ordinary
school the instruction should cluster round the
parent stem and never get far away from the
common stream of English speech.

Those who write on the more attractive aspects
of English are wont to set up at the outset a
barbed-wire fence; for they begin by warning
off all those who do not know grammar. Wherein

they differ from the writers of books on physical science; for they lure the student by assuring him (falsely in nine cases out of ten) that no knowledge of mathematics on his part is pre-supposed. Fifty years ago Abbott and Seeley wrote an excellent little book called *English Lessons for English People*. But the opening words of the Preface were : " This book is not intended to supply the place of an English Grammar. It presupposes a knowledge of gram-mar and of English idiom in its readers." These words shut the book out of most schools and scared off the plain man, the soldier, the sailor, the apprentice and the ploughboy, whom Cobbett invited to read his *Grammar*. And yet no tech-nical knowledge of grammar is really needed to understand the book and to profit by its teach-ings. For one large section deals with the deriva-tion of words, another large section deals with figures of speech, and the largest section of all (about a third of the book) deals with versifica-tion. This predilection for grammar as a pro-pædeutic is, no doubt, due to the mistake of thinking that what is logically prior is also pedagogically prior. As a child uses parts of speech before he uses figures of speech, it is assumed that he should be taught parts of speech before he is taught figures of speech. But what really should determine the sequence of studies is the development of interests in the child's mind. And if it is true (as I believe it is) that a child is interested in figures of speech before he is interested in parts of speech, figures of speech should be taught first, whatever grammarians and logicians may say to the contrary.

I am now treading on uncertain ground. No investigation has ever been made into the ages at which the various parts of Rhetoric can profitably be taught; nor has any been made into the effect of such teaching on the pupils' attitude towards literature. And many minds must work at the problem and much time must pass before we can arrive at anything like certainty on these matters. It is certain, however, that literature is the life, the soul, the spirit of English teaching; literature in its double aspect—the studying of English classics and the practice of English prose; and if there be no time for other things, then other things must go. But if there be time (and there generally is), some branch of Rhetoric should be taught. And in choosing the branch the sole criterion should be its effect on the study of literature. If it vitalizes and vivifies that study, increasing its hold and influence on the pupil's mind, it should be adopted with gladness; but if, on the other hand, it deadens his interest in great literature and makes the expression of his thoughts in speech or essay an irksome task, then it should be mercilessly shut out.

It is clear that verse should be practised; not to make the pupils poets, but to make them lovers of poetry—discriminating lovers of poetry; to give them a sense of literary form, through experience of working under self-imposed limitations, and of being compelled to weave a double pattern of rhyme and rhythm without at the same time writing nonsense. One thing at least they will discover: they will discover how easy it is to write bad poetry. The importance of prosody (a branch of study included in most grammar-books and excluded from most curricula) demands a chapter to itself. That the chapter is missing from this book is due to the smallness of my experience either in training children to write verse or in seeing them so trained.

When we have discovered what branches of Rhetoric it were wise to teach, we must consider how to set about teaching them. We must not deceive ourselves with the facile phrase: " Teach it incidentally "—a phrase that may mean anything or nothing. A young teacher once tried to teach the multiplication table incidentally during a lesson in oral composition. The topic was: " A Stitch in Time saves Nine," and she asked the class to tell her how many two stitches in time would save. Referring to grammar as

an abstract science, Dr. J. H. Jagger says tersely :
" You can no more teach grammar incidentally
than you can teach astronomy incidentally."

I have urged that as the pupil gets older he
should acquire a critical attitude towards the
products of his own mind ; but this critical
attitude is not without its dangers. One danger
is that he should attach too much importance
to verbal accuracy—that in his preoccupation
with the letter the spirit should escape him.
The cardinal importance of thought, on which
such stress has been laid in this book, is neatly
expressed by Quintilian in a maxim that appears
in Blair's *Lectures on Rhetoric : Cura sit verborum ;
solicitudo rerum.* Freely paraphrased this means :
Be careful of your words ; but be doubly careful
of your subject-matter.

The other danger that besets the path of the
young critic is that criticism should pass into
censure ; not of himself (that would not matter),
but of other people. He should be reminded (if
necessary) that criticism is intended to be used,
not as a weapon of offence, but as a preserver of
the integrity of the mother tongue ; he should
be reminded, too, that there are other things
which are better than even grammar and literary
taste. Common kindness and courtesy, for instance. Between the lad who would botanize on
his mother's grave and the lad who would correct

his grandmother's grammar, there is not much to choose.

After all is told, more importance must be attached to the spirit in which the teacher takes up the teaching of English than to the details of subject-matter or the details of method. If the spirit be generous and humane, all will be well. This generous spirit pervades many recent writings on the subject; particularly Professor Adams's chapter on *English* in *The New Teaching*, Dr. F. H. Hayward's *Lesson in Appreciation*, and the finely humane writings of the late Mr. Hardress O'Grady. I attach importance to this spirit because the pupil is ever exposed to its contagion. And what he unconsciously catches of its grace and charm sinks more deeply into his soul than anything he consciously learns from the teacher's lips, or gleans from the printed page.

INDEX

PRINTED IN GREAT BRITAIN BY RICHARD CLAY & SONS, LIMITED,
PARIS GARDEN, STAMFORD ST., S.E. 1, AND BUNGAY, SUFFOLK.

THE NEW TEACHING SERIES

HISTORY AND ENGLISH

Citizenship
By F. R. WORTS, M.A.   4/6 net

"A careful and valuable book . . . attractively written by a skilled teacher of the subject."—*Times Educational Supplement.*

The Light of History
By K. W. SPIKES   4/6 net

"An interesting and accurate . . . sketch of nineteen hundred years of European history . . . evidence of extensive reading, fresh ideas and balanced judgment.'—*Journal of Education.*

Modern Industrial History
By F. R. WORTS, M.A.   4/6 net

"Can claim to have fulfilled its purpose of informing and encouraging the student who begins this fascinating and interesting study."—*Schoolmaster.*

An Introduction to World History
By E. H. SHORT   4/6 net

"A masterly monograph on a great subject."—*Education.*

English Literature : The Rudiments of its Art and Craft
By E. V. DOWNS, B.A.   4/6 net

"Good, modern, and even fascinating. The exercises are useful, though sometimes daring."—*Educational Times.*

GEOGRAPHY

Geography of Commerce and Industry
By R. S. BRIDGE, M.A.   4/6 net

"The book is a real romance . . . it is also a mine of information . . . no student of modern economics should fail to read it. It is essentially a book for the times."—*Education.*

The Natural Wealth of Britain
By S. J. DULY, B.A.   6/- net

"The book is one to be read by all teachers of geography, who should find inspiration from the author's novel outlook."—
Journal of Education.

HODDER AND STOUGHTON, LTD., LONDON.

THE NEW TEACHING SERIES

MATHEMATICS

Everyday Mathematics
By F. SANDON, M.A.   4/6 net
". . . Succeeds in a wholly praiseworthy effort to get out of the text-book groove. The subject is made really interesting from start to finish."—*Educational Times*.

Mathematics of Business and Commerce
By O. H. COCKS and E. P. GLOVER   4/6 net
"The requirements of the average student of the commercial section of the continuation schools have been constantly kept in view. The book bears out this statement in an admirable way."—*System*.

Foundations of Engineering
By W. H. SPIKES, B.A.   4/6 net
"It is part of the value of a work of this kind that the ordinary reader can follow the development of engineering and arrive at a clear understanding of the 'reasons why.'"—*Athenæum*.

Pure Mathematics: With Special Reference to Engineering
In two volumes. **By S. BARRINGTON GATES, B.A.,** sometime Wrangler and Scholar of Corpus Christi College, Cambridge.   4/6 net each

PART I. includes Algebra, Trigonometry and Geometry ; PART II. the Calculus Analytical Geometry and General Curves. One feature of the work is its remarkable conciseness. The text is lucid and some of the examples are of special value to engineers.

SCIENCE

Applied Botany
By G. S. M. ELLIS, M.A.   4/6 net
"One of the best introductions to botanical science that we have seen. Mr. Ellis has, in a high degree, the inevitable gift of a simple, very readable style."—*Journal of Botany*.

Chemistry from the Industrial Standpoint
By P. C. L. THORNE, M.A.   4/6 net
"An interesting little book on a very large subject, which is clearly and attractively explained, and the volume marks a considerable departure from the older style of text-book."—*Nature*.

HODDER AND STOUGHTON, LTD., LONDON.

THE ROMANCE OF BRITISH INDUSTRY

THE problem of most practical men and women is that of acquiring what, in modern knowledge, will be for them equivalent to the "humanities" so dear to their more leisured forebears. Time and opportunity are so limited, and the task of choosing what is vital in the mass of human wisdom is so immense, as to present almost insuperable difficulties.

With the coming of the Day Continuation School in England this problem has to be faced ; for the "young persons" who attend these classes are engaged in industry and have very little time at their disposal. The "Romance of British Industry Series" is a thoughtful and ingenious attempt to solve the problem.

The dominant British industries are made the medium, for they are of vital interest to every citizen of the Empire. Each industry has its roots in history, its extension in geography, and its flower in literature. Each volume, therefore, unfolds the story of industry in such a way that the "English Studies"—history, geography and literature—become a unity of humane study.

The student learns the true place of industry in the history of mankind, he learns how to trace the influences which have been exercised by geographical factors, he learns something of the extent to which industry has found expression in art and literature, and he is helped to appreciate his own significance in the general scheme of things.

Each volume is illustrated, and contains many exercises for the student, whether it be the drawing of a map, the making of an illustrative chart, or the construction of a model.

Now Ready. 2/3 net each

The Tools of Man	By John Hill
Man and Wool	By Ernest H. Short
Man and Commerce	By R. S. Bridge
Man and Cotton	By Ernest H. Short

HODDER AND STOUGHTON, LTD., LONDON.

SOME IMPORTANT BOOKS ON THE NEW PSYCHOLOGY PUBLISHED FOR THE UNIVERSITY OF LONDON PRESS, LTD., BY HODDER AND STOUGHTON, LTD., LONDON

Education for Self-Realisation and Social Service

A Text-book for Class Teachers in the Psychology of Human Development. By F. WATTS, M.A. (London), Lecturer in Experimental Psychology, Manchester University, and in the Department of Industrial Administration, Manchester College of Technology, with wide experience in elementary school work, and author of "Echo Personalities." Crown 8vo. Cloth. 7/6 net.

This volume covers the increasingly important matter of the psychology of the class as a miniature of society.

The Education of Behaviour

By IDA B. SAXBY. With Illustrations. Crown 8vo. Cloth. 6/- net.

This is a book on psychology written for teachers and those training as teachers. The special merit of the book is the skill with which it applies recent psychological advances to the needs of the educator. The author is a lecturer at the University College of South Wales and Monmouthshire.

Psychanalysis in the Classroom

By GEORGE H. GREEN, B.Sc., B.Litt. Crown 8vo. Cloth. Probably 7/6 net.

The author has made a very wide study of his subject, and all his conclusions are based upon practical experience.

Mind and Work : The Psychological Factors in Industry and Commerce

By CHARLES S. MYERS, M.A., M.D., F.R.S., etc., Director of the Psychological Laboratory, Cambridge University; Member of the Industrial Fatigue Research Board, etc. With Illustrations. 6/- net.

"Admirably concise and convincing."—*The Morning Post.*

"We can cordially recommend this book and feel that it has a wide sphere of usefulness."—*British Medical Journal.*